The Preparation of Teachers
of Brain-Injured Children

The Preparation of Teachers of Brain-Injured Children

WILLIAM M. CRUICKSHANK

JOHN B. JUNKALA

JAMES L. PAUL

SYRACUSE UNIVERSITY PRESS

Syracuse University
Special Education and Rehabilitation
Monograph Series 8

William M. Cruickshank, *Editor*

The project reported in this monograph was
supported by the National Institute of Mental Health,
under Mental Health Training Grant MH–7559,
and by Syracuse University.

ABOUT THE AUTHORS

During the period of the project each of the authors was associated with the Division of Special Education and Rehabilitation of Syracuse University.

WILLIAM M. CRUICKSHANK, Ph.D., is presently Professor of Psychology, Department of Health Development, School of Public Health; Professor of Psychology, College of Literature, Science and the Arts; Professor of Education, School of Education; and Director, Institute for the Study of Mental Retardation, The University of Michigan.

JOHN B. JUNKALA, Ed.D., is Associate Professor of Special Education, Boston College, Boston, Massachusetts.

JAMES L. PAUL, Ed.D., is Senior Education Consultant, North Carolina State Department of Mental Health, Raleigh.

PREFACE

Gilbert Highet in his volume, *The Powers of Poetry,* speaking of other matters, has succinctly characterized the problem of the brain-injured and hyperactive child: ". . . the conflict between fragmentation and incoherence on the one hand, and stability and poise on the other. . . ." It is the responsibility of the professions that are concerned with the problem to assist the brain-injured child to overcome inner fragmentation and to develop stability and poise.

This volume reports the results of a demonstration program conducted at Syracuse University during the years 1961-67, for the training of teachers of brain-injured and hyperactive children. The basic concepts for the training program were derived from earlier studies made by the senior author.

The education of brain-injured and hyperactive children requires the teacher to focus on the disability while keeping in mind all the needs of the child. As a physician must treat a specific ailment, so the teacher of exceptional children must concentrate on a specific disability in order to help the child to function satisfactorily.

To accomplish this, and to provide teachers with an understanding of their role in the process, special teacher education programs will have to be developed which go beyond the limits of general elementary education. The program reported here brought to light many problems of administration in this type of special education that directly affected the results achieved by the teachers, and largely determined the success or failure of the program in individual schools.

The authors hope that this report and the discussion of the problems they encountered will be of assistance to educators at all levels in the field of special education for brain-injured and hyperactive children. The book presents the realities faced in attempting innovative procedures, both in the universities where training must

be undertaken and in the schools in which these children will have
to be served.

W.M.C., J.B.J., J.L.P.

Ann Arbor, Michigan
May 1, 1968

ACKNOWLEDGMENTS

The authors are indebted to many persons who over the five-year period of this teacher preparation project devoted much time and energy to its completion. The school systems which sent teachers to the University for preparation provided the project personnel with great freedom in visiting the systems after the teachers returned, and in evaluating and assessing the effectiveness of the programs once they were established. To these public school officials the authors are grateful. The forty-seven teachers who participated in the four training classes must also be recognized. Unusual and rigorous demands were made during the year they spent at the University and, with little more than the expected resistance when fatigued, the teachers met every demand and request with good nature and cooperation.

The list of those persons who actively participated in the program is long. Chief among these are the following:

Peter Knoblock, Ph.D., Associate Professor of Special Education, Syracuse University, who not only participated in teaching important strands of the program, but who also served as a psychological consultant;

Gene L. Carey, M.D., Assistant Professor of Psychiatry, State University of New York College of Medicine, Syracuse, who served as a psychiatric consultant;

Miss Ruth Cheves, M.S., now Assistant Professor of Special Education, University of Houston, upon whom rested the major responsibility for teacher preparation insofar as methods and materials were concerned;

Mrs. Pauline Stanley, M.S., Teacher, Syracuse City School District, who served as demonstration teacher for three years;

Eva Woolfolk, Ph.D., Assistant Professor of Special Education, and Mr. Edward Brower, M.S., who served as psychologists with the project at different times;

Eleanore Westhead, Ph.D., now of the University of Virginia, and David Lema, Ed.D., now of the University of Pacific, who at various times were responsible for follow-up and evaluation;

Andrew Shotick, Ph.D., now of the University of Georgia, who assisted the senior author in originally developing the program and who during its first three years actively supervised and coordinated the entire program;

Bernice Kipfer, Ed.D., and her predecessor, Miss Isa M. Cole, who as heads of the department of Special Education in the Syracuse City School District, made possible the development of a special class for demonstration purposes. The superintendent of schools, Dr. Franklyn Barry, and assistant superintendent of schools, Dr. Edwin Weeks, were particularly helpful with administrative and business details related to this class;

Mr. Nile Hunt, M.S., Director of Instructional Services, North Carolina State Department of Education, and Mr. John Pelosi, M.A., M.S., Rehabilitation Lecturer, Syracuse University, who were kind enough to read the manuscript, and offered invaluable reactions and suggestions for chapters 1 through 4;

Miss Saroj Sutaria, Ph.D., now of Kent State University, graduate assistant for the final two years of the project, who with her quiet competence saw to the numberless details which form such an important part of any undertaking of this scope.

Numerous medical and psychological diagnosticians from Syracuse University and from the State University of New York College of Medicine in Syracuse were helpful many times during the course of the four years of work with children.

Many faculty members from Syracuse University made special plans for the more satisfactory preparation of the teachers included in this program. In this connection, Dr. John Wilson, should be particularly mentioned.

To all these the authors are greatly indebted and extend their thanks.

Parents of the children were cooperative throughout the project in providing much data and in making themselves available for study and observation, to the end that the teachers could obtain a better understanding of the nature of the learning and adjustment problems.

During the four years of teacher preparation, graduate students in the Syracuse University School of Social Work were assigned to the project as a field placement. They performed many valuable services, working directly with both parents and children. Their work is recognized by the authors, as is the valuable help received from faculty members of the School of Social Work, Mrs. Hortense S. Cochrane, Professor of Social Work, and Mr. Warren G. Augins, Assistant Professor of Social Work.

Appreciation is also extended to the officials of the Syracuse University Research Institute who made many services available to the authors and

ACKNOWLEDGEMENTS xi

to the project without which only partial success could have been achieved.

The authors especially wish to acknowledge the creative and unstinting assistance rendered by their secretary, Mrs. Marion Merica.

W.M.C., J.B.J., J.L.P.

CONTENTS

TABLES

FIGURES

The Preparation of Teachers
of Brain-Injured Children

CHAPTER I

Introduction

Thirty years ago this book could not have been written. Fifteen years ago it might have been considered. Today it is written, but in another fifteen years it will have to be rewritten with new facts and new points of view. The education of brain-injured and hyperactive children is a field which is fluid in nature at present. It is too soon to say that any one orientation—educational, psychological, or psychiatric—contains all the elements for understanding these children, and we feel that an interdisciplinary approach to education of these children is essential. One approach to the preparation of teachers of brain-injured and hyperactive children is described here, but other approaches to this complex field may also be valid and should be tried.

As recently as 1940, only a very few professional educators expressed any concern whatsoever about the brain-injured child, or those who function like them but are often called hyperactive or hyperkinetic children, and one can almost count on the fingers of two hands the number who were making serious attempts to provide special attention for these children. Lauretta Bender [1], concerned with problems of organicity in children, was making significant strides toward a better understanding of them by 1940, and Heinz Werner and Alfred A. Strauss, co-workers at Wayne County Training School in Michigan, were engaged in a series of important investigations concerned with psychopathology in exogenous mentally retarded children. In close relation to this field of child development, Kanner [2] was investigating and reporting on the unique behavior of autistic children. Bradley [3] was studying schizophrenia in childhood, and was adding pertinent information from another area. Others could be named, but their number is surprisingly limited. In neurology, Penfield and Rasmussen [4] were contributing information to the problem, while Phelps [5], working with cerebral palsy children was, from his orthopedic vantage point, stimulating interest concerning that complicated neuro-educational problem. These forerunners of professional activity, however, were but a few of the numbers needed to investigate the problems thoroughly. Their significant writings and public addresses, along with their personal encouragement of their colleagues and young research associates served, thirty years ago, as the beginning of what is now developing into a huge national and multi-disciplinary effort.

At the close of World War II and during the decade of the 1950's, research momentum increased, particularly in psychology and education, resulting in a greater understanding of the problems of the brain-injured child. Parents, individually and in groups, began to express a serious concern about the appropriateness of the education which their handicapped children were receiving in the public schools. Teachers were perplexed by the responses which certain children made to their instructional programs, and as professional persons they began to make inquiries into the reasons for this. These children were often looked upon as being emotionally disturbed, as behavior or management problems, or as children who were developmentally immature and who probably should have been kept in an earlier grade for another year. But it was found that when these children were held back they still did not learn. Maturity and increased chronological age did not appear to have the same impact on their learning ability as it did on others. The efforts made by teachers to help them failed to produce results commensurate with the energy expended. This awareness on the part of teachers began to be expressed to the profession with increased vigor, and serious attention began to be given to the problem.

As of the writing of this monograph, there are undoubtedly few other areas of disability in children which receive such extensive attention as does that of brain injury. Parents are organizing themselves into groups capable of sponsoring educational, diagnostic, and treatment programs; national organizations are devoting their funds to research; federal health agencies have assumed a leadership role in research and in stimulating professional preparation in many fields; all of the major disciplines have outlined significant efforts in behalf of these children, and many of these efforts have already accomplished much. Other plans are either projected or are being undertaken. A vital and healthy flood of research, professional inquiry, and discussion can be observed on all sides, and gradually, as a result of these efforts, a logical understanding of the brain-injured and hyperactive child is being achieved. There is still a long way to go, however, before full realization of the total problem is possessed by all who should be concerned with it.

PREVIOUS RELATED ACTIVITIES

The authors are aware of the vast amount of literature which already exists relative to general education. They are aware also of the ample literature pertaining to teacher education in the field of special education. In the interest of space, however, we have decided merely to recognize the existence of this related research and literature [6] and to assume that it is already within the perspective of the thoughtful reader. Only those previous publications which are directly pertinent to the philosophical orientation of the authors, and which were either forerunners of the present study or resulted from it, will be mentioned here. While there are other studies dealing with teacher preparation in one field or another of special education, little has been published which deals specifically with the education of teachers for brain-injured children.

In making this decision the authors realize that they are ignoring the significant writings of Kephart [7], Frostig [8], Barsch [9], Rappaport [10], Gallagher [11], and many others. These will be referred to when appropriate, but no one of them is solely concerned with teacher education. In addition to these important authors there must be added the names of Haeussermann [12], Taylor [13], Gardner [14], Reitan [15], Haring and Phillips [16], Rubin, Simpson and Betwee [17], Benton [18], Rabinovitch [19], Bateman [20], and a long list of other contemporary writers and investigators whose publications add to the literature. Each of these authors deals with related topics, but does not concentrate on the field of the preparation of teachers for brain-injured children.

Two teacher education programs in this field must be mentioned. Marianne Frostig has for several years been engaged in teacher education at the Frostig Center for Educational Therapy in Los Angeles. Although this school makes its major effort in the provision of direct services to children, Dr. Frostig, recognizing that well-prepared teachers are required for brain-injured and perceptually handicapped children and that her Center provides an excellent setting for this preparation, has added a graduate program of teacher education in recent years. Similarly, at Purdue University, Dr. Newell C. Kephart has combined teacher education with his service-oriented diagnostic and research program in the University's Achievement Center for Children. Both of these programs were initiated at about the same time as the one at Syracuse University which is reported in this volume.

Very little was available in the literature in 1955, and no formal studies had been undertaken which were concerned with the education of brain-injured children. The important publication of Strauss and Lehtinen in 1947, which had grown out of the research of Werner and Strauss, was concerned with psychopathology and education of brain-injured children, not with teacher education *per se*. Nothing had been written at that time about the problem of teacher education for children of this type, and little of major significance was done in this field for some years.

In 1957, through funds received from the Cooperative Research Program of the U.S. Office of Education, a joint project was initiated by Syracuse University and the Montgomery County Public Schools, Maryland, to determine some of the practical problems related to a specialized technique for the education of brain-injured and hyperactive children [21]. This project, one of those alluded to earlier, was originally initiated as a five-year program. However, because of a variety of factors operating at that time, chiefly within the government funding office, funding of this project was curtailed and the project was discontinued at the end of the second year. Thus, although much of significance was learned, many factors which would have been important to the education of these children and indirectly to teacher preparation could either not be reported or had been studied for too short a period of time to be conclusive. An investigation of this area of education which has extended over a sufficiently long period of time to make conclusive statements possible is yet to be completed.

The Syracuse-Montgomery project, however, contained several important elements. Among these was the multidisciplinary diagnostic program established for the screening and admission of children to the educational program. Experienced professional personnel representing special education, psychology, pediatric neurology, pediatric psychiatry, pediatrics, audiology and speech pathology, ophthalmology, optometry, and general elementary education each examined a large number of children who had earlier been screened out of the elementary school population. Multidisciplinary staff conferences were held, the aim of which was to obtain unanimity, if possible, regarding the diagnosis of brain injury and hyperactivity in the child. The significant value of the multidisciplinary approach for education became evident immediately, and important understandings of the problems of this approach as it pertained both to services to children and to the ultimate requirements for teacher preparation were observed and obtained.

Forty children were included in the four classes organized in the Syracuse-Montgomery project. No university or college in the United States at that time was preparing teachers specifically for these children, that is, within a context consistent with the authors' point of view. Since this was to be an educational project which depended basically on the sophistication of the classroom educator, the problem of the appropriately trained teacher had to be resolved at the outset. Other major issues also had to be faced by the investigators. The forty children were being served by twenty-seven private pediatricians and many of these children, as private patients, were then on prescribed programs of medication for the control of hyperactivity. A wide variety of medications was being employed, introducing a variable which was uncontrollable without medical cooperation.

The staff pediatrician, in cooperation with the private practitioners, was successful in having all medication suspended (except that required in a few cases for the control of seizures) for one academic year, in order that the educational program variable alone could be studied and controlled. A similar cooperative arrangement was made with several pediatric psychiatrists who were treating some of the children psychotherapeutically. Thus, external variables were controlled as much as possible in order that the impact of teaching and educational programming could be ascertained.

The problem of teachers untrained insofar as specialized techniques were concerned still remained. The County educational system, by the usual standards, had more than its share of skilled educators. From a group of recommended personnel, four teachers (two for the experimental classes and two for the control classes) were carefully selected, who appeared to have the personality characteristics believed to be required for the type of teaching which was to be projected. These teachers, together with two non-professional teacher assistants, were provided an intensive six-week summer orientation relative to the education of hyperactive and brain-injured children. This was continued for a second summer and would have been continued for a longer period of time had not the program terminated at the end of the second academic year. As with the problem of multidisciplinary diagnosis, this minor venture into teacher education provided the authors with much information regarding the problems related to the unique features of teacher education in this complicated aspect of child development. The observations which were made of teacher performance and of teacher understandings during the two-year educational project were, in large measure, the latent factors which became important later in a more formal approach to the preparation of teachers of brain-injured and hyperactive children.

It is important at this point to reiterate what already has been said, namely, there has never been a study completed which has lasted over a sufficiently long period of time to permit a full understanding of the value of any educational regimen with brain-injured or hyperactive children. The Syracuse-Montgomery project certainly indicates some important avenues for educational research and for practical educational programming. It was neither extensive enough nor sufficiently longitudinal in nature to provide more than a professional sensitization to the problem. However, pressures were beginning to build up nationally from parents and professional groups to initiate and extend these educational programs. Direction was needed, and in spite of the limited nature of the Syracuse-

Montgomery project, the senior author was approached by representatives of the National Institute of Mental Health in 1961, following the publication of the report of the earlier project, to ascertain his interest in giving leadership to further exploratory activities concerning teacher preparation in this same field. On the basis of insufficient experimental data, but in the face of demands for service, an educational program for teacher preparation was projected. It is thus safe to say that in a decade or two, as more knowledge about these children is obtained, much of what has been written in the past decade by the senior author of this volume will indeed need to be amplified by more definitive information. That this would be welcomed by the present writers cannot be overemphasized.

Historically, the education of brain-injured and hyperactive children presents different problems from those of any other field of special education insofar as teacher education is concerned. In other related areas, teacher education has been a matter of professional concern for many years, and a few teachers have been graduated each year from colleges and universities in a small but steady stream since about 1920. College and university personnel have been comfortable with the nature of the programs which were available, and have had many precedents upon which to depend. Professional activity, while not entirely adequate, nevertheless was on the record. Furthermore, what was offered had preceded the tremendous force of parental activity by many years. Hence, when parents became sufficiently aroused to produce changes, colleges and universities were prepared to act on at least a minimal basis, to reorganize, and to enlarge their programs for increased student enrollment and service.

These efforts did not include the brain-injured and hyperactive child. No programs in institutions of higher education existed at the time parents began to organize themselves for effective action. Parents were ahead of the professionals. Certainly they were ahead of research and of practically every other aspect of this complicated problem in their realization that a problem existed and must be solved. Parent action, then, created a pressure which professional people hastened to try to meet, but in doing so they lacked both information and any precedent from the past history of other fields of special education. Confusion thus existed on all sides and continues to exist, for, since 1957 and the beginning of the Syracuse-Montgomery program to this date, relatively little has happened to fill the gap between parental pressures and knowledgeable teacher preparation.

Looking at the problem objectively, it can be stated that the Syracuse-Montgomery project has been significant in helping to give direction to practical educational programming for brain-injured children. As with so much which goes on in special education, however, many programs which have been initiated as a result of the project must of necessity operate on a theoretical base rather than from an experimental one. It is interesting, however, to note that in the absence of experimentation most of the writing which has appeared relating to the education of brain-injured children approaches the matter from the same general orientation as that of the writers. If there is safety in numbers, then on this premise one might feel secure in taking the next steps. It will be useful to examine some of the collateral writings which are available.

Related Literature

The publication of Strauss and Lehtinen [22] has been referred to previously. So much has been written about the contribution of Werner and Strauss that it would be inappropriate here to again discuss this matter. Suffice it to say that beginning about 1940, Heinz Werner and Alfred Strauss entered into a professional compact, the result of which was a series of important papers [22] dealing with the psychoneurological and psycho-educational characteristics and needs of exogenous mentally retarded children. These authors identified the fact that mental retardation, insofar as education was concerned, was not a matter of homogeneity, but rather that within the large population of mentally retarded children there were two unique and distinct groups of children. (The authors actually designated six clinical groups, but only two of these are of concern in this report.) It was indicated that the psychological and learning characteristics of exogenous (brain-injured) mentally retarded children differed from those of endogenous (familial) mentally retarded children to the extent that quite different educational approaches were undoubtedly required to meet the needs of the two groups of children. While Werner and Strauss were unable to carry out long-term educational programs which produced quantified information with exogenous children, they did engage in sufficient clinical teaching with these children to make possible the educational generalizations which appeared in the 1947 publication of Strauss and Lehtinen. This publication is based completely on the Werner-Strauss research. Lehtinen also indicates the educational implications of the psychopathology characteristic of the exogenous child and demonstrates appropriate educational procedures to be used. The importance of this document cannot be in any way minimized, for it has given form to almost all of the subsequent writing and research which has been done in this broad field of childhood disability.

It must be restated that the work of Werner and Strauss was limited to mentally retarded children. It appeared to the senior author of this monograph, however, that much of what was discussed in relation to exogenous mentally retarded subjects was also typical of many cerebral palsy children. For this reason, a preliminary study of this latter type of child was launched in 1948 by Dolphin and Cruickshank [24]. The purpose of this investigation was to determine whether or not cerebral palsy children of normal intelligence were characterized by psychopathology similar to that identified by the earlier investigators in exogenous mentally retarded children.

Although the Dolphin study was exceedingly limited in scope, it did serve the function of a pilot investigation. It did indicate that characteristics similar to those observed by Werner and Strauss were present in the cerebral palsy children. This pilot study led to a much larger one in 1957 conducted by Cruickshank, Bice, and Wallen [25] (later extended and reported in 1965 by Cruickshank, Bice, Wallen, and Lynch [26]) which employed a more adequate sample of chidren from the point of view of size and clinical accuracy. Athetoid and spastic cerebral palsy children were compared with physically normal children, and numerous clinical characteristics of psychopathology, similar to the earlier ones reported, were statistically confirmed. Shortly after the Dolphin study, Shaw [27], another student of Cruickshank, undertook an investigation of the psychopathology inherent in an undifferentiated group of epileptic children with similar results. Norris [28] and Trippe [29] followed these studies with those of additional clinical populations of deaf and cerebral palsy children, and added further pertinent information. Within the Syracuse University group of studies, all clinical populations had been characterized by some type of central nervous system disorder.

Haring and Phillips [30], as late as 1962, reported on a study in which they utilized emotionally disturbed children and approached them educationally from the same standpoint as the previously mentioned authors, namely, from an educational frame of reference based upon work with brain-injured and hyperactive children as reported by Cruickshank *et al.* This was the first time that the early concepts of Werner, Strauss, and Lehtinen had been applied to a group not specifically identified as having some type of neurological disorder, although the possibility that some of the children in the Haring and Phillips group were indeed neurologically involved as well as emotionally disturbed was not ruled out by the latter authors. The Haring and Phillips program adhered closely to that described in the 1961 Syracuse-Montgomery report to which they had had prepublication access.

Kephart's volume appeared in 1960 [31]. Kephart had at one time been associated with Werner and Strauss at the Wayne County Training School, and it is safe to say that his interest in the brain-injured child and children who demonstrate special learning problems was stimulated and molded by the work of the latter two men. His volume, while more inclusive and more extensive than the earlier work of Strauss and Lehtinen, nevertheless approaches the problem of psychopathology and education of the brain-injured child from a point of view nearly identical to that held by the original investigators and that of the present senior author.

It is also important to note Gallagher's report, which appeared in 1960. While the Syracuse-Montgomery study was concerned with small groups of brain-injured children who were of essentially normal intelligence, Gallagher [32] reported on a study which utilized a tutorial approach with mentally retarded brain-injured children. The educational approach he used, however, was essentially the same as the one employed in the Syracuse-Montgomery study. The point being made here is that throughout the short history of the education of brain-injured children there has been a largely consistent theoretical approach taken by a variety of authors. Obviously, individuals from different professional backgrounds approach the problem from the orientation of their profession and training. The writings of Bender [33] and Eisenberg [34] view the problem from a psychiatric and sometimes psychoanalytic point of view, those of Rappaport [35] and Frostig [36] approach the brain-injured child from the point of view of ego psychology, and Gallagher views the problem from the perspective of educational psychology. There is a surprising degree of agreement among authors, however, in spite of their different professional backgrounds, and the emphasis on theoretical consistency within the professions is stressed here because of the absence of any substantial amount of experimental data.

Finally, the second of the major publications to which reference was earlier made is the one dealing with competencies required of teachers of brain-injured children which appeared in 1966 [37]. This volume, comprised of significant papers prepared by leading personnel in the field of brain injury, again indicates a degree of basic consistency in point of view. While differences in approach to the brain-injured child are observed from one writer to another and from one profession to another, there are more areas of general agreement than there are significant theoretical differences.

SEMANTICS

The semantic variant in this disability area has been noted in other publications [38], but will again be commented upon briefly. The Syracuse-Montgomery report refers to "brain-injured and hyperactive" children. All of these children, however, demonstrated the classical characteristics of psychopathology which have been described many times. These authors prefer to continue with the utilization of these terms in the present monograph, both to provide consistency in their publications, and because this is undoubtedly accurate in terms of the children who are involved. There is little value in repeating the arguments in favor of the utilization of these terms in opposition to more than forty others which appear in the literature. Brain injury is used here as a hypothetical construct. It is recognized at present that neither educational, psychological, nor neurological instrumentation is sufficiently sensitive to be able to determine the presence or absence of brain injury in every instance. This factor has not been of great concern to these writers. The important factor is that, irrespective of terminology, children grouped for educational purposes must have common psychological characteristics. If this is not accomplished, teachers will not be able to achieve much with the children in their charge no matter how excellent their preparation. When instrumentation is developed which is sufficient to the need, it is felt that the hypothesis of brain injury will be borne out with the vast majority of children now labeled: hyperactive, dyslexic, children with special or specific learning problems, exogenous, hyperkinetic, children with maturational lag, or any one of a variety of different labels. In the majority of instances, these are children who have most likely experienced brain injury at some stage of their early development, prenatally, perinatally or postnatally. Until we have adequate clinical diagnostic tools, educators seeking to serve these children will have to rely on grouping the children according to psychopathology, not according to medical-clinical classifications, and will have to design educational programs specific to the pathology which is indicated. The preparation of teachers of brain-injured and hyperactive children, as it is reported in this volume, is predicated on this point of view.

TEACHER PREPARATION AND MEDICAL LABELS

The history of formalized teacher preparation in special education goes back to the summer of 1918 when Charles Scott Barry, then at the Lapeer State Home and Training School in Michigan, organized a small summer program for teachers of mentally retarded children. This program operated in cooperation with Charles M. Elliott at what was then known as the Michigan State Normal School (now Eastern Michigan University). It was the beginning of what is now a large and diversified series of programs in many universities and colleges throughout the United States and in other countries. The preparation of teachers in certain fields of disability also had its beginning in residential schools, in particular those serving the deaf and the blind.

Teacher education in all fields of special education prior to 1940 was essentially a matter of transmission from one generation of teachers to another of the important techniques and methods which had been found helpful to the earlier group. Practically nothing in any field of special education was predicated on experimentation or carefully controlled research. The education of the mentally retarded children was characterized chiefly by handicrafts and minor modifications of what was thought to be appropriate for intellectually normal children, and teacher education in this field reflected these attitudes.

In spite of the lack of experimental data upon which to base either teacher education or childhood education of handicapped children prior to 1940, the public schools nevertheless made many attempts to provide educational services. Almost all clinical types of handicapped children were served by the public schools, although admittedly not always with the best educational tools.

After 1940, particularly since World War II, more and more of special education has been premised on better and better research data. The amount of money which has been invested in educational research in the various fields related to special education, while less than in some scientific fields, is nevertheless very great. New techniques and new understandings based upon research findings are coming into the classrooms for the deaf, the crippled, the blind, the mentally retarded and for other groups of children with physical, intellectual or social disabilities.

Teacher education, likewise, has changed much insofar as content is concerned. Teacher education should, if indeed it has not, reflect the findings of the research laboratories even before the children's classroom does. Unfortunately, although some gains have been made, they fall short of the best which colleges and universities should be doing.

The brain-injured and hyperactive children have not been identified as a group requiring special services at any point in the history of the development of teacher education in special education until very recently. These children have not been adequately served at any point in the educational history of the United States, and still are not receiving the services which they must have in order to take their places in society as contributing members.

In addition to the problems within the field of teacher education *per se,* there has been another matter which has retarded progress toward maximum quality in special education programs. Throughout the entire history of special education, and even today, handicapped children have been grouped together according to long-standing medical and clinical classifications. Special education has been organized around the blind as a group, around the deaf, the hard-of-hearing, the crippled child, the epileptic, the mentally retarded (or feebleminded), the speech-handicapped, the emotionally disturbed, and other clinical groupings. Teacher education has likewise been organized around these same concepts. Teachers are certified in most states in terms of the clinical group which is to be served, i.e., as a teacher of the blind as opposed, until recently, to a teacher of the partially sighted.

We have already pointed out how Werner and Strauss suggested that within the category of mental retardation there existed at least two distinct educational problems: the endogenous and exogenous. Teachers of special education have long recognized what superintendents of schools, education professors and certification personnel have failed to realize; namely, that within the neatly conceived clinical organization of children there were many who failed to respond to the best teaching which could be provided. Teachers who approached the mentally retarded children in their classes with the most appropriate methodology at their command were rewarded by the failure of a certain percentage of their children to respond, and who often appeared to regress. Teachers of cerebral palsy children recognized, without understanding the dynamics of the problem, that methods of education appropriate for most of their children simply did not produce the desired results with others. Teachers of blind children were frequently perplexed by the failure of certain intellectually well-endowed children to learn to read braille. Teachers of deaf children, even when the so-called "aphasic group" was removed from their responsibility, were still perplexed by the failure of some children to respond to good educational methodology. The perplexities of teachers regarding this problem over the years are still characteristic of them today, in spite of the fact that different organizational patterns have been suggested.

The basis of the problem is that, although children are grouped according to medical classifications, this does not produce homogeneity. Within the categories of the deaf, the blind, the mentally retarded, or the cerebral palsied there will be many children whose behavior and learning characteristics generally follow that of normal children. These may well be grouped according to the traditional procedures. In each of the groups, however, there will be a large number of children whose learning is characterized by psychopathology typical of those children who have identifiable central nervous system disorders. These characteristics have been described too often elsewhere to be repeated again. Suffice it to say that characteristics such as short attention span, distractibility, perseveration, figure-background reversal, dissociation, and deficient self-concepts, individually or together in varying degrees of significance, preclude the child's achievement when taught in the traditional educational environment and by traditional teaching methods. Aberrant behavior and disengaged or dysfunctional learning processes should be the primary targets of psychoeducational strategies.

A child with an attention span of approximately two minutes will not be able to realize success in a typical grade group if the reading, arithmetic, spelling, and other lessons are organized for periods of approximately twenty minutes. A child who is characterized by figure-background reversal may never learn to read if reading materials typical of those presented to normal children are used, regardless of the fact that his measured intelligence may be within or above normal levels.

It is interesting to observe that culturally disadvantaged children, perhaps the newest group of children to be identified, are immediately thought of as a homogeneous group. We hear competent educators speak of "teachers of culturally disadvantaged children," or of "urban school teachers," implying that if one can arrange to have a whole class of culturally disadvantaged children brought together under the skills of a teacher of culturally disadvantaged children all problems will be solved. Remarkable degrees of individual differences, some of them closely akin to those of brain-injured children, also typify this group of children. It is difficult to see how an adequate educational program can be launched for disabled children of any type if educators continue to perpetuate outworn medical or sociological models.

It may be useful to make a distinction between two processes which characterize our efforts to understand children. One, we may call describing; the other, explaining. If the two, not being mutually exclusive, can be seen in relation to a continuum, the behaviorist is more oriented to the description of behavior while the more psychodynamically oriented person is concerned with explanation. There is a basic philosophic difference in the attitude toward man and in what one is willing to call real. Explanation is an attempt to deal with cause or, basically the question of *why*, going beyond what is clearly visible. The physical sciences have been able to do this with some precision. The social and behavioral sciences usually have to rely upon basic assumptions, unproved by definition.

The medical model, which includes the concept of symptomatology (description) and can be understood in relation to disease, abnormal growth, accidents, or other factors (explanation), has often been applied in the social and behavioral sciences without examining the assumptions which accompany it. Szasz [39] has discussed some of the difficulties in transplanting models. There does not seem to be any point in elaborating upon this issue or discussing in great detail the technical and philosophical points of cause and effect. The point is that while we can reach some consensus in describing behavior and characteristics of performance, much of our currently used classification system is devised from etiological or explanatory premises. An adequate taxonomy based on behavioral (descriptive) categories has not been derived. We only need to note that extreme caution should be exercised in dealing with the implications of some of our clinical designations, particularly when our purpose is to plan an educational program. We obviously need to continually refine and redefine our attempts at explanation. Here we make specific our own philosophic positions and belief and, consequently, give direction and interpretation to a particular strategy. This is the level which remains most vague and, of course, constitutes the area of most variance of opinion.

We have suggested in the earlier pages of this chapter that it is possible to assess a child's characteristics so carefully that a clear-cut blueprint of him can be obtained. This means more than merely identifying the mental age or the intelligence quotient, and a listing of the child's strengths and weaknesses relative to his mental age. These factors are important, of course, but the problem goes much further than this. It is possible to know the extent to which the attention span of the child is limited; it is possible to know whether sensory hyperactivity is present and in what degree it exists with relation to a given sensory modality; it is possible to ascertain whether a child perseverates, reverses field, dissociates, or functions in an incoherent manner; it is possible to determine if the child possesses a distorted body-image and an immature self-concept. Children who demonstrate these problems can be placed together in very small groups for instruction, irrespective of their medical problem. They are grouped according to the presence of psychopathology, the issue with which educators must be concerned.

There are limitations to this insofar as the variance of medical problems is concerned. The authors have had no experience in grouping hyperactive blind children with hyperactive deaf children, and it is assumed that it would be inappropriate to do so. However, it would be appropriate to separate the blind children into at least two groups; those whose learning problems are characterized by psychopathology, and those whose learning problems are typical of the norm. Identical statements can be made for any of the traditional groups in special education. The authors have, however, had experience in grouping children on the basis of their psychopathology, and these groups contained some children who, for example, had specific diagnosis of brain injury, others who were hyperactive without evidence of brain injury, some who were intellectually normal or above, and others who were characterized by degrees of mental retardation. A teacher of broad background was provided for these children, one with preparation in the specific methods of teaching to the disability, and who understood and could obtain the specialized teaching materials necessitated by the psychopathology with which the children had to deal. Under such conditions, these children have made progress. They have learned, in contradistinction to their previous performance when they were members of regular elementary education classes or special education classes organized around traditional medical concepts.

A clinical type of teaching is required in this situation. It is a situation which is predicated on the concept of one-to-one teaching, and it is firmly based in an understanding on the part of the adult of the nature of the individual differences and needs represented in the children who are being served.

How many such children there are is unknown at present. It has been stated on many occasions by the senior author that these children are undoubtedly to be found in every elementary school of the nation, and are probably to be found in almost every classroom in every elementary school. Certainly there are several such children in almost every special class group in the country. One is hesitant to speak of these children in terms of percentages, for any figure given at present would be nothing more than an educated guess. Percentages of from one to seven are frequently heard, any of which would result in a sizable problem for educators. It is assumed by these writers that the problem is a large one, and that in size it ultimately may indeed be found to approximate that of the endogenous mentally retarded group. Careful studies of incidence and prevalence need to be completed with large segments of the school population in order that educators may ascertain the magnitude of the problem in reality. It is certainly larger than can be adequately served in the years immediately ahead, and it is the area of the greatest shortage of teachers.

There is, however, a much more crucial problem to be solved before teachers can be prepared: *the preparation of college professors who have a full grasp of the nature of the problem, who have had sufficient experience with research, and enough direct contact with these children to make instruction in colleges and universities meaningful.* Until there is a well-qualified corps of university professors, teacher education cannot go forward in any consistent or effective pattern. Until teachers are available, children cannot be served. Since the possibility of obtaining this corps of college professors is obviously still in the future, brain-injured and hyperactive children are not likely to be served in any large numbers for many years to come. This is a tragic situation in American education, and it cannot be permitted to continue indefinitely. The availability of college professors for future teachers of brain-injured and hyperactive children today is comparable to that in the total field of special education in 1940. Thoughtful persons are now educating themselves in whatever way seems appropriate in order to meet the emerging need represented within their educational institutions, and the efforts of these people will help in overcoming this critical shortage of teachers, but this informal approach is not what the profession needs or deserves. A more consistent program is essential, and a crash program is needed immediately.

Teacher education in this field is faced with some sizable problems: the lack of a defined population, the lack of knowledge of its actual size, the unavailability of college professors, the inadequacy of traditional grouping procedures, and the lack of sufficient teaching materials for use with the children. These are significant hurdles. On the other hand, children who can definitely be identified as being children in need are now present in the schools. Every teacher and school principal can identify them without too much effort. These children have to be served. The failure to serve them means a continuance of family and classroom disorganization, tensions, and unhappiness. It means that children continue to grow into adolescence without the skills for appropriate social adjustment; it means that emotionally disturbed children in increasing numbers characterize the leaving group who depart annually from public schools; it means that many individuals enter the community as young adults without the techniques for realizing their inherent potential. The economics of our culture can ill afford this. It cannot be allowed to continue.

Teachers skilled in the education of children with brain injury and emotional disturbance, singly or in combination, must be prepared for the public and private schools which seek to serve these children and their families. It was in this sense, as we have earlier stated, that representatives of the National Institute of Mental Health approached one of the authors in 1961 to ascertain his interest in projecting a teacher education program and in trying to determine its effectiveness.

The story of this development will be related in this monograph. It will be a straightforward account of the problem which was faced, how it was undertaken, the nature of the individuals who participated, and their experiences subsequent to the close of the training program. The authors have felt that it was essential to present here the strengths as well as the weaknesses of the program in the hopes that a full accounting would assist others in other universities to build stronger programs.

The report of the present teacher education program includes an important extension, namely, an evaluation of the university program insofar as its impact on local school systems is concerned. The evaluation phase originally was intended to be restricted to the specific classes which university-prepared teachers began in their local school districts following the completion of their training program. This was soon extended to become also an appraisal of the local school district factors which expedited or impaired effective new programming. A university teacher education program which is meant to provoke new thought, research, diagnostic procedures, and practice ought to be an instrument for change. The evaluations which have been undertaken here encompass those things in the local school system which affect the potential for change, but school systems and personnel working in them will not be identified specifically. It may be that, in the future, techniques can be developed within the profession of education generally, and within special education particularly, which will take into account some of the problems of program implementation and thus minimize them in terms of effective educational services for children.

REFERENCES

1. Lauretta Bender, *Psychopathology of Children With Organic Brain Disorders* (Springfield, Ill.: Charles C Thomas, 1956).

2. L. Kanner, "Autistic Disturbances of Affective Contact," *Nervous Child*, II (1943), 217–50.

3. C. Bradley, *Schizophrenia in Childhood* (New York: The Macmillan Company, 1941).

4. W. Penfield and T. Rasmussen, *The Cerebral Cortex of Man* (New York: The Macmillan Company, 1950).

5. W. M. Phelps, *Education in Cerebral Palsy* (Chicago, Ill.: National Society for Crippled Children and Adults, Inc., pamphlet, prior to 1946).

6. The interested reader will find an extensive bibliography pertinent to teacher education generally and to special education particularly at the end of the book.

7. N. C. Kephart, *The Slow Learner in the Classroom* (Columbus, O.: Charles E. Merrill Books, Inc., 1960).

8. Marianne Frostig, *et al.,* "A Developmental Test of Visual Perception for Evaluating Normal and Neurologically Handicapped Children," *Perceptual and Motor Skills,* XXII (1961), 383–94.

9. R. Barsch, "The Concept of Regression in the Brain-Injured Child," *Exceptional Children,* XXVII (1960), 84–89.

10. S. R. Rappaport, (ed.), *Childhood Aphasia and Brain Damage: A Definition* (Narberth, Pa.: Livingston Publishing Company, 1964); S. R. Rappaport (ed.), *Childhood Aphasia and Brain Damage,* Vol. II, *Differential Diagnosis* (Narberth, Pa.: Livingston Publishing Company, 1965).

11. J. J. Gallagher, *The Tutoring of Brain-Injured Mentally Retarded Children* (Springfield, Ill.: Charles C Thomas, 1960).

12. Else Haeussermann, "Evaluating the Developmental Level of Pre-school Children Handicapped by Cerebral Palsy," *Journal of Genetic Psychology,* LXXX (1952), 3–23.

13. Edith Meyer Taylor, *Psychological Appraisal of Children with Cerebral Defects* (Cambridge, Mass.: Harvard University Press, 1959).

14. R. Gardner, "The Development of Cognitive Structures," *Cognition: Theory, Research, Promise,* ed. Constance Scheerer (New York: Harper and Row, 1964).

15. R. M. Reitan, "A Research Program on the Psychological Effects of Brain Lesions in Human Beings," *International Review of Research in Mental Retardation,* Vol. I, ed. N. R. Ellis (New York: Academic Press, Inc., 1966).

16. N. G. Haring and E. L. Phillips, *Educating Emotionally Disturbed Children* (New York: McGraw-Hill Book Company, Inc., 1962).

17. E. Z. Rubin, C. B. Simson, and M. C. Betwee, *Emotionally Handicapped Children and the Elementary School* (Detroit, Mich.: Wayne State University Press, 1966).

18. A. L. Benton, *Right-Left Discrimination and Finger Localization: Development and Pathology* (New York: Paul B. Hoeber, Inc., 1959).

19. R. D. Rabinovitch, "Reading and Learning Disabilities," *American Handbook of Psychiatry,* Vol. I, ed. Silvano Arieti (New York: Basic Books, 1959), chap. 43.

20. Barbara Bateman, "Learning Disabilities: Yesterday, Today, and Tomorrow," *Exceptional Children,* XXXI (1964), 167–77.

21. W. M. Cruickshank, Frances A. Bentzen, F. H. Ratzburg, and Mirian T. Tannhauser, *A Teaching Method for Brain-Injured and Hyperactive Children,* Syracuse University Special Education and Rehabilitation Monograph Series 6 (Syracuse, N.Y.: Syracuse University Press, 1961).

22. A. A. Strauss and Laura E. Lehtinen, *Psychopathology and Education of the Brain-Injured Child,* Vol. I (New York: Grune and Stratton, Inc., 1947).

23. A. A. Strauss and H. Werner, "The Mental Organization of the Brain-Injured Mentally Defective Child," *American Journal of Psychiatry,* XCVII (1941), 1194–1202; A. A. Strauss and H. Werner, "Experimental Analysis of the Clinical Symptom 'Perseveration' in Mentally Retarded Children," *American Journal of Mental Deficiency,* XLVII (1942), 185–87; A. A. Strauss and H.

Werner, "Impairment in Thought Processes of Brain-injured Children," *American Journal of Mental Deficiency*, XLVII (1943), 291–95; H. Werner and A. A. Strauss, "Pathology of Figure-Background Relationship in the Child," *Journal of Abnormal and Social Psychology*, XXXVI (1941), 236–48; H. Werner and A. A. Strauss, "Problems and Methods of Functional Analysis in Mentally Deficient Children," *Journal of Abnormal and Social Psychology*, XXXIV (1939), 37–62.

24. J. E. Dolphin and W. M. Cruickshank, "The Figure-Background Relationship in Children with Cerebral Palsy," *Journal of Clinical Psychology*, VII (1951), 228–31; J. E. Dolphin and W. M. Cruickshank, "Visuo-Motor Perception in Children with Cerebral Palsy," *Quarterly Journal of Child Behavior*, III (1951) 198–209; J. E. Dolphin and W. M. Cruickshank, "Pathology of Concept Formation in Children with Cerebral Palsy," *American Journal of Mental Deficiency*, LVI (1951), 386–92; J. E. Dolphin and W. M. Cruickshank, "Tactual Motor Perception of Children with Cerebral Palsy," *Journal of Personality*, XX (1952), 466–71.

25. W. M. Cruickshank, H. V. Bice, and N. E. Wallen, *Perception and Cerebral Palsy*, Syracuse University Special Education and Rehabilitation Monograph Series 2 (Syracuse, N.Y.: Syracuse University Press, 1957).

26. W. M. Cruickshank, H. V. Bice, N. E. Wallen, and Karen S. Lynch, *Perception and Cerebral Palsy*, Syracuse University Special Education and Rehabilitation Monograph Series 2 (2d ed.; Syracuse, N.Y.: Syracuse University Press, 1965).

27. M. C. Shaw, "A Study of Certain Aspects of Perception and Conceptual Thinking in Idiopathic Epileptic Children," Unpublished Doctoral Dissertation, Syracuse University, 1955.

28. H. J. Norris, "An Exploration of the Relation of Certain Theoretical Constructs to a Behavioral Syndrome of Brain Pathology," Unpublished Doctoral Dissertation, Syracuse University, 1958.

29. M. Trippe, "A Study of the Relationship Between Visual Perceptual Ability and Selected Personality Variables in a Group of Cerebral Palsied Children," Unpublished Doctoral Dissertation, Syracuse University, 1955.

30. Haring and Phillips, *op. cit.*

31. Kephart, *op. cit.*

32. Gallagher, *op. cit.*

33. Bender, *op. cit.*

34. L. Eisenberg, "Behavioral Manifestation of Cerebral Damage," *Brain Damage in Children: The Biological and Social Aspects,* ed. H. G. Birch (New York: The Williams and Wilkins Company, 1964).

35. Rappaport, *op. cit.*

36. Frostig, *et al., op. cit.*

37. W. M. Cruickshank (ed.), *The Teacher of Brain-Injured Children: A Discussion of the Bases for Competency,* Syracuse University Special Education and Rehabilitation Monograph Series 7 (Syracuse, N.Y.: Syracuse University Press, 1966).

38. *Ibid.*

39. T. Szasz, *The Myth of Mental Illness* (New York: Hoeber-Harper, 1961).

CHAPTER II

A Plan for Teacher Education

In 1961 there were no colleges or universities in the United States
which were formally preparing teachers of brain-injured and hyperactive children. There were no guidelines of previous programs in
higher education which could serve as models. This was probably
good, for it prevented what Samuel A. Kirk has often referred to
as the "cafeteria approach" to teacher education from being employed with the group of teachers being reported upon here. The
task was to devise a new and intensive program of teacher education which would provide experienced teachers with the understanding, insights, and teaching skills to make it possible for them to
develop programs of education of a high level of professional
sophistication for children who were hyperactive and brain-injured.
To accomplish this, funds were received to permit a teacher education program of four years' duration, with an additional year to be
used for the final post-training evaluation.

THE PLAN

The arrangements which were made within the university were
not unusual, and they were purposely kept within the financial
capacities of most colleges and universities. Under the conditions
of the grant, funds for scholarships were available which might not
ordinarily be a part of the typical university budget, but an attempt
was made to keep the preparation program within the usual financial resources of a university. This is not, however, an aspect of
teacher education which should be undertaken by small colleges or
those of limited financial means. The costs of special education are

23

great at best, and the preparation of teachers of brain-injured and hyperactive children is undoubtedly more costly than in some of the other aspects of special education.

The plan was to recruit twelve teachers a year for four years, admit them to a graduate school of education in residence for one year, provide an intensive program of specialized teacher preparation during this time, and return them to their school systems to begin classes for brain-injured and hyperactive children the following year. Following their return to their school districts, personnel from the project staff in the university would visit each class to evaluate the impact of the specialized training on the educational programs of the schools. The Division of Special Education and Rehabilitation of Syracuse University was the co-sponsor of this project in cooperation with the National Institute for Mental Health. The senior author of this monograph was the project director.

SELECTION OF TEACHERS

Initially, superintendents of schools were approached by letter or directly by the project director with a description of the proposed program. Obviously, approaches were made to public school systems in which some interest in the problem of the education of brain-injured or hyperactive children had been shown. In many of the cooperating systems one or another of the university faculty, the project director, or others had served as consultants or were in some way directly aware of the professional concern for these children. Officials of these school systems were invited to send one or more teachers to the program.

The school system was to be obligated to place the teacher on leave of absence for one year at half-salary. The project funds provided a scholarship or training grant of $4,500 for each teacher out of which university tuition was to be paid. With some exceptions, the school systems paid the teacher a half-salary which, together with the training grant, meant that the teacher could live in reasonable comfort and devote her entire attention to the activities involved in the program. No teachers were permitted to accept employment in addition to the grant, as this would have been practically impossible in terms of the work load within the project for which each teacher was responsible. In one or two instances the board of education paid the full salary of the teacher in addition to the grant, on the premise that the teacher had financial obligations in the home community which had to be maintained during her absence on leave.

The school system assumed the responsibility of making whatever arrangements were deemed necessary to insure that the teacher returned to the system for a period of time following the completion of the university program. This was essential in terms of post-training evaluation and in terms of other factors to be mentioned. (As a matter of fact, the university officials involved in the project took the initiative in two instances to insist that the teacher return to the sending school district on the premise that this was part of the original contract into which the school system, the teacher, and the university had entered.)

The project personnel furnished the school superintendent with some guidelines for the selection of the teachers. On an *a priori* basis it was felt, for example, that teachers who were to work with these difficult children and with these equally difficult educational problems must have had some previous experience with children, so it was stated that teachers to be sent to the university should have had a minimum of four years of successful experience. It was suggested that this experience should be at the elementary school level, although this was not an absolute in the selection process. The definition of what "successful experience" should be was left to the discretion of the public school officials. The minimum of four years was an arbitrary decision as well. Experience, however, was desired.

It was also indicated to the superintendent that teachers were sought who possessed certain characteristics. Whether they were to be men or women was of no consequence, since both sexes were felt to be needed in the program. Superintendents were asked to select teachers who were known to be patient with children and who were known to be creative. Those who were not shocked by unusual language or child behavior were more acceptable than those who might find it necessary to impose rigid rules of behavior and who were inflexible in their attitudes about social standards. Since the methods of teaching and the teaching materials which were to be advocated were known to be different from those customarily employed in elementary education, it was necessary to secure teachers for the project who were willing to set aside conventional techniques with which they were familiar and to try something which might appear to them to be completely foreign to "good" educational practice. Teachers who could see the value of slow progress in children and be content with it were more desired than those whose personal satisfactions required marked and immediate evidence of achievement. Superintendents were cautioned to select teachers who were known to be well-adjusted, emotionally secure, and who possessed personalities which were acceptant of children and which inspired a reasonable degree of confidence in children. These were the criteria upon which superintendents were asked to base the selection of their candidates.

Since this was a graduate program, each teacher must have completed a baccalaureate degree, thus requiring each to meet the minimum standards for admission to the graduate school of education. These included the quality of the undergraduate transcript, an acceptable score on the Miller Analogies Test, and appropriate letters of recommendation. University personnel attempted to get an assessment of the teachers through sources in the communities which were mutually familiar with both the teacher and the university, but this was not possible in many instances. These were the criteria. The extent to which they were successful in bringing together an outstanding group of teachers will become obvious in later pages of this monograph.

THE ADMINISTRATORS' SEMINAR

Although the nature of the administrators' seminar will be discussed more fully later, it had a bearing on the selection of teachers and on the ability of the school system to participate. It was felt by the university personnel that teachers, though often well-prepared and professionally sophisticated, were unable to initiate appropriate programs for children because of a lack of understanding of the programs on the part of the administrators of the school system in which the teacher was employed. Since the education of brain-injured and hyperactive children is exceedingly complicated and involves much administrative understanding, it was felt that, in order to insure some degree of success and to warrant the unusual investment which was being made by a government agency, the matter of administrative understanding had to be considered. School systems were therefore invited to participate in the program and to send one or more teachers if it could be assured that the administrator to whom the teacher would be responsible upon her return to the school system the following fall would also be sent to the university for a seven-day period to attend a professional seminar. The school system was required to underwrite all expenses of the administrator during the seminar except for lodging and meals while in Syracuse, New York. The school system could, if it desired, send more than one administrator, but in this case the system had to assume all expenses for the additional personnel. On several occasions, in addition to the school principal in whose building the program was to operate, school systems also sent a psychologist, a director of guidance or pupil personnel, an assistant superintendent, or some other school official.

When the school administration accepted the conditions and was able to select a teacher who supposedly possessed the desired characteristics, the teacher then applied to the University to determine whether or not she [1] met the admission requirements. When all these details were satisfied, the teacher entered the program and continued in it for a ten-month period, September through June.

In addition to the factors which have been mentioned regarding teacher selection, the sending school districts were required to state in writing that, upon her return to the district, the teacher would be allowed to use the new methods in a manner in keeping with the additional preparation she had received in the program. As the reader will note in the following sections, classroom teachers were selected by the districts and were admitted to the university program in practically all instances. Exceptions were granted in two cases. In these, individuals were admitted when it was known that upon their return to their district they would function in supervisory or consultative roles in relationship to the development of programs for brain-injured and hyperactive children. Thus, over the four-year period, forty-seven educators were selected by their school districts (one Catholic order sent two teachers) to participate in the program and to prepare themselves to become teachers in this specialized field. In one instance, one teacher was permitted to renew the grant and to participate in the program for a second year.

THE PHILOSOPHICAL ORIENTATION OF THE PROGRAM

It had been the observation and experience of the project director that often, in spite of what appeared to be good programs of teacher preparation, new teachers arrived in a classroom without any definite orientation of educational beliefs. Upon consideration of this fact, it was assumed that the failure of teachers to have a total understanding of their program or a real commitment to it was due to the fact that at no time in their preparatory period were they introduced to it in sufficient detail to allow them to feel free to take a single point of view. This results in the trial-and-error approach so characteristic of new teachers, and also of many who have taught for longer periods of time. Educators, to their disadvantage, tend to be too cautious and too concerned with the fear of criticism to strongly advocate any one school of thought. This hesitancy characterizes much, if not all, of the preparatory aspects of teacher education. Students are exposed to numerous philosophies or to what is considered to be an eclectic point of view which cuts across the surface and snares the "best" of numerous points of view. This technique too often fails to provide the student with sufficient depth of understanding of any one point of view to enable him to comprehend its significance or to understand the basis for including portions of the philosophy (while ignoring others) in the eclectic schema. It is for this reason that teachers can seldom defend their point of view with full assurance that they truly understand the fundamentals inherent in it.

It was determined that within the short period of time available to the present program it would be impossible to engage in a sufficient number of dialogues with the students to permit a full understanding of the several points of view and the several schools of thought which might apply to the education of brain-injured or hyperactive children. With this in mind, an arbitrary decision was made to pursue a thorough understanding of a single point of view for the entire year, so that when the teachers left the university to return to their classrooms they would be in complete command of the theoretical structure, the teaching method, and the details of its implementation. They would thus be able to function comfortably within it and be able to discuss it rationally with colleagues to whom it might appear foreign or unusual. The teachers were informed of this decision during a period of orientation on the first day of the seminar. While the single theme ran throughout the year and everything within the program was related to it, care was taken to ascertain that the teachers were exposed to other points of view to provide them with a basis for comparison. To obtain this fuller perspective, consultants representing other philosophical orientations were invited to participate in the seminar. There was a conscious recognition by the presenting faculty that theirs were different points of view which were being presented for comparative purposes, not from the point of view of eclecticism. All students also were members of a course taught by a faculty member known to have a point of view different from that of the project director. In these and other ways, care was taken to assure breadth and extensive exposure to much of the total field of education of exceptional children while, at the same time, major emphasis was being placed intensively on a single concept.

The point of view which was stressed during the year was that previously advocated by the project director in earlier writings, namely, a structured approach founded upon a concept of contiguous conditioning [2] and developed from a detailed analysis of the psycho-educational deficits which characterize the child [3].

Insofar as possible, recognizing the problem of human variables in understanding and practice, this philosophy and teaching method was stressed in the theoretical discussions of the seminar, in the techniques of the teaching method and materials used, in the demonstration class, the tutorial sessions, and the motor training program. It was thus possible for a teacher-in-training to become quite conversant with all of the details of the method. She could leave the year of training with a thorough understanding in depth of at least one way of dealing with brain-injured and hyperactive children. She could have a sufficient grasp of the method to thoroughly understand what she was doing and to understand rationally what was happening, or might happen, when she modified the procedure in one way or another in her own classroom.

The authors are satisfied that the decision which has just been described was an appropriate one and that, with minor modifications, it would be repeated in future programs. In order to reduce variables as much as possible throughout the four years of the program, plans initiated during the first year with Class I were continued with all the classes, even though there was a recognition of both strengths and weaknesses in certain areas of the program. Some details were modified as time went on, but the program for Class I was essentially the same as that of Class IV.

THE ACADEMIC PROGRAM OF THE UNIVERSITY

In order to accomplish the program, a sequence of courses and experiences within the masters degree requirements of the graduate school of education was planned. Several teachers arrived at the university who had already obtained such a degree elsewhere. In some instances, a second masters degree was planned for them; in others, the teacher entered an advanced graduate program and sought a Certificate of Advanced Study. In one instance, a student preferred to utilize this year as part of the university's requirements for the doctor of education degree, which she intended to pursue and complete after returning to her school system for a period of time. Essentially, however, the program was conceptualized by the project personnel as a masters degree program, and will be identified here as such.

At Syracuse University the masters degree involves a minimum of 30 semester hours of credit, and this minimum was accepted for the project program because of the large number of clock hours per week which would be required for related professional activities.

The program was divided into two parts in keeping with the university requirements: foundation or core courses, and courses specific to the field of specialization. The former accounted for 9 semester hours in three courses; the latter, 21 semester hours.

Core courses

a. A course in educational philosophy, comparative education, or history of education pertinent to the student's interest and background: 3 semester hours.

b. A course in educational measurement or statistics: 3 semester hours.

c. A course in child or adolescent psychology which was selected by the student not only in terms of her background and interest area, but in terms of the chronological age level of the children with whom she would be working the following year: 3 semester hours.

Specialization courses

Some selection was permitted among these courses, particularly where courses would duplicate other graduate studies which had been accomplished elsewhere. The list of courses noted below, however, is essentially that which characterized the study programs of the teachers. It also must be pointed out that this list of courses changed somewhat from year to year as the university faculty changed, and as it became apparent that certain courses were more pertinent than others for individual teachers. In several instances, university faculty members offered special sections of their courses whose membership consisted only of the project teachers. In this way, instruction could be made more specific and more realistic insofar as the interests and needs of the teachers were concerned.

a. A course in the psychology of disability. This was a general course dealing with the psychological problems of children and youth who were characterized by a wide variety of intellectual, physical, and social disabilities. It was a one-semester course: 3 semester hours.

b. A course in the education of emotionally disturbed children. This was a two-semester course with special sections limited to the project personnel: 6 semester hours.

c. A course in the diagnosis and treatment of reading problems: 3 semester hours.

d. A course in the diagnosis and treatment of arithmetic problems: 3 semester hours. (These latter two courses were utilized only when the teacher's previous preparation showed a deficiency in one or both areas. On occasion, teachers selected these courses in addition to the minimum of 30 semester hours.)

e. Seminar in the education of brain-injured and hyperactive children. This was a full year course limited to the project personnel, and was valued at six semester hours credit one semester; three, the second, although the actual number of clock hours required of the teacher varied only slightly throughout the year: 9 semester hours.

The formal course aspect of the program culminated in a one-day examination at the end of the academic year. This examination consisted of two parts: a half-day examination in the foundations areas, and a half-day examination in the specialized area. It would be inappropriate here to discuss the contents of each of the specialized courses in detail. Suffice it to say that professors of each course were consulted by the project staff members to make sure that the lectures, reading, and field experiences which were planned for the courses were related as closely as possible to the goals of the project teachers, and several faculty members organized special sections of their courses for these teachers in order to bring their information more directly to bear on the problems which the teachers were preparing themselves to face. It is a compliment to the cooperating faculty that a wide variety of subject matter and related activities pertinent to the problems of the brain-injured and hyperactive child were developed especially for the participants of the program. It was, however, in the seminar on the education of these children that the most intense effort was made on topics directly related to the problem at hand. For this reason, special discussion will be included outlining the many aspects of this seminar.

THE SEMINAR PROGRAM

The seminar constituted the major focus of the project. Although it was assigned a credit-hour value in the university system, this was considered as a minimum in planning activities which would center in the formal aspect of the seminar and others which would grow out of it and be related to it. The planned program occupied approximately twenty to thirty clock hours of the teachers' time per week in specified activities, in addition to the actual time required in formal seminar sessions. Almost all of the other courses were scheduled during the late afternoon or evening hours, thus leaving the whole day free for seminars. The following activities were among those integrated into the seminar program during the course of the ten-month period.

THEORY AND METHODS

The seminar members met as a formal unit for a four-hour period once a week. Two hours of this time for several weeks were spent in a formal presentation by the project director of the major characteristics of psychopathology in brain-injured and hyperactive children. This responsibility was assigned to William M. Cruickshank, Ph.D., Professor, Syracuse University. This didactic phase included a historical summary of the research pertinent to psychopathology in exogenous mentally retarded children, and the related findings as they have appeared in the literature on cerebral palsy, epilepsy, emotional disturbance, psychosis, and other types of disability and mental illness. Considerable emphasis was placed on the clinical methods of determining psychopathology. Finally, the educational implications of psychopathology insofar as teaching environment, classroom physical arrangements, daily programming, and teaching materials were concerned was discussed and demonstrated.

Basing her work upon these discussions, a second university faculty member, Miss Ruth Cheves, Lecturer, Syracuse University, met the group for the second two-hour period each week to discuss the details of the teaching method, the materials of teaching, and problems of classroom management. This phase of the program continued throughout the ten-month period, often taking up considerably more time each week than the scheduled seminar period. Detailed information pertaining to reading, number concepts, visuo-motor training, motor training, handwriting, spelling, language development, discipline, informal recreational activities, and pupil-teacher relationship was provided during this phase, along with opportunity for discussion. The reader is here referred to a collateral source for a detailed description of the nature of this part of the program: W. M. Cruickshank, *The Brain-Injured Child in Home, School and Community* (Syracuse: Syracuse University Press, 1967, chapters 6–10, incl.). This volume was an outgrowth of the project and contains a detailed description of the contents of the syllabus which was used in these two portions of the seminar.

What is now recognized as having been an inordinate amount of outside preparation was required of the teachers on assignments related to the theory and methods phase of the seminar. During the early weeks of the program many volumes of related literature were assigned for immediate reading and this was continued during the first half of the total program. Extensive files were maintained by the students related to teaching materials and techniques. The teachers-in-training were required to make teaching materials in large quantities, so that when they returned to their school systems they would have available models of almost everything which might be needed by them during the first year of their teaching experience with brain-injured and hyperactive children.

The didactic phase of the seminar also included other types of formal presentations by cooperating consultants, and with few exceptions the same consultants returned year after year to meet with each group of teachers.

1. Gene L. Carey, M.D., State University of New York College of Medicine, Syracuse, a pediatric psychiatrist, was employed as a permanent member of the project staff as consultant. A part of his responsibilities included four two-hour sessions each year with the teachers in which basic psychiatric concepts relating to brain injury and emotional disturbances were presented. The consultant also served as a psychiatric resource for the staff demonstration teacher. He participated in staff conferences, and periodically examined each child in the demonstration class. He thus knew the entire program in great detail and was able to integrate into his formal lectures much of the reality behavior and adjustment problems of a group of children whose members were also well known to the project teachers.

2. Miriam Pauls Hardy, Ph.D., Professor, Speech Clinic, Johns Hopkins University Medical Center, Baltimore, Maryland, spent one full day each year in lecture and discussion with the teachers.

In effect, more than a day was spent with the teachers, as the consultation began at dinner the evening before and continued into the evening, giving the students the opportunity to become familiar with the personality and ideas of the consultant before the formal presentation began. These consultative visits were limited to the group of twelve teachers in each annual program in order to insure that these teachers would have ample time to listen, to question, and to discuss with each consultant-visitor, and in order that the consultant's attention would not be diverted to problems which went beyond the scope of the project. Each consultant prepared detailed reading lists, and on some occasions, position papers, which were provided to the students, and these were used in predetermined ways.

3. A second consultant who spent an evening and full day with the group each year was Fritz Redl, Ph.D., Wayne State University, Detroit, Michigan [4]. Dr. Redl was included in the group because he represented a somewhat different orientation to psychopathology and behavior in childhood than that which was being presented to the students as the major orientation of the teaching method.

4. Sheldon R. Rappaport, Ph.D., The Pathway School, Norristown, Pennsylvania, participated as a consultant in the same manner as did Dr. Hardy and Dr. Redl, stressing his orientation to the brain-injured child, founded essentially in concepts of ego psychology [5].

5. Ruth Newman, Ph.D., of the Washington School of Psychiatry, Washington, D.C., participated in the consultant series twice during the four-year period stressing in particular the dynamics of the Life Space Interview [6] as a technique of behavior control effective in the classroom.

6. William C. Morse, Ph.D., Professor, The University of Michigan, attended the consultant series during each of the four years to discuss with the teachers the issues of classroom management and emotional disturbance [7].

7. Paul Lewis, O.D., Silver Spring, Maryland, met the teachers annually as a part of the series to describe for them programs of visuo-motor training which are appropriate to the total educational program for brain-injured and hyperactive children.

8. Ruth M. Lencione, Ph.D., participated in the series three times in the four years. As Associate Professor of Speech Pathology, Syracuse University, she particularly stressed the normative development of speech as a basis for teacher understanding of the deviations in speech and language production in brain-injured and hyperactive children.

9. E. Harris Nober, Ph.D., Associate Professor of Audiology, Syracuse University, was concerned with discussion of normal hearing for a similar purpose.

10. During each year of the four years of teacher education, a clinical psychologist was appointed to the staff. Three different persons filled this position during the four years, but each had received the same type of professional preparation and each had received his orientation to the brain-injured child from the project director. Hence, uniformity in point of view was maintained over the four years although personnel changed. During the seminar, the clinical psychologist met with the teachers for a minimum of three two-hour sessions for detailed discussion of certain measurement techniques which were being recommended for utilization by the teachers in the classroom. The clinical psychologist also carried on periodic evaluations of the children in the demonstration class and participated in staff conferences, thereby allowing the didactic aspect of the seminar presentation to be integrated easily into the classroom management program which the teachers were observing daily.

11. A social work trainee on field assignment was assigned to the project each year. During some periods there were two social work trainees assigned to the project at the same time. These persons were all very mature, and each had had extensive previous experience with emotionally disturbed children. They performed invaluable services under supervision. The social worker was scheduled to meet with the teachers for one two-hour period each year to discuss the function of a social worker in the public school setting, and the nature of the contribution which the social worker can make in relation to brain-injured children and their families. The social worker's impact on the program, however, was much greater than this, for he was present part of each day in the building where the major program was conducted. He observed the

children, worked with their parents, and participated in the staff conferences. The teachers were thus able to see how this professional person carried out his responsibilities in relationship to a school program.

12. Physicians from the State University of New York College of Medicine in Syracuse representing neurology, pharmacology, pediatrics, and other specialties related to the education of brain-injured and hyperactive children, attended the teachers' seminars and spoke on assigned topics. The personnel varied from year to year but, in general, the topics covered by these representatives remained the same throughout the four classes.

In addition to the position papers which several consultants prepared, each consultant was furnished with a list of questions prepared by the teachers in advance of his arrival. These lists of questions provided some idea of the scope of the teachers' interests and the nature of their professional concerns. Typical of the discussion questions which were prepared for the consultants are the following three sets:

Questions prepared by Class I for Dr. Fritz Redl:

What specific help can the teacher expect from the psychologist in order to facilitate a more effective program of instruction?

Physical restraint or contact has been suggested as a means of controlling, reassuring and defining boundaries for hyperactive, emotionally disturbed children. Are there children to whom physical contact and restraint may be upsetting or threatening?

If the teacher is expected to be "all things to all students" can our "educational therapy" be effective for all types of disturbed children, or does this suggest a continuum in the amount of disturbance that may be handled in all day classrooms or residential settings?

How do you view "structure" in the classroom?

Can you suggest a method for resolving the conflicts between "middle class" values that many teachers possess and the behavior they are facing with many of the disturbed children?

How do you differentiate between "limit-setting situations" and "threats" in the classroom?

There is often an ambivalence in the feelings a teacher may have toward the behavior of a child and the verbal reassurance she gives to the child. Can't the child sense this? At this time, is it better to exclude the child?

Questions prepared by Class II for Dr. Ruth Newman:

How and when can a teacher in the self-contained classroom, with all her obligations and responsibilities to her entire class, utilize the techniques of the Life Space Interview?

How can the teacher know when the child is simply adjusting to the situation itself, because it's the "easiest" way, rather than really beginning to understand himself and his problems? Motivation?

What preparation should a teacher have if she desires to use the Life Space Interview techniques?

What should a teacher do or say when she discovers, while getting to the basis of a child's behavior in school, that the incident causing the disturbance acted only as a trigger to some deeper problem that had developed beyond the teacher's sphere of influence?

When the child exhibits values that differ from the school's values, how should the teacher cope with this situation?

What effect do peers in a classroom of emotionally disturbed children have on the individual child in the class?

What characteristics should a child exhibit who appears too sick for any classroom learning?

What is the teacher's role in the emotionally disturbed classroom? Educator? Therapist?

What viewpoint do you hold concerning structure in the classroom? (Administration)

Is it psychologically sound to isolate a child from the group when he is not behaving?

How can a school be oriented to the positive acceptance of a hyperactive, emotionally disturbed classroom?

Without psychological resources at hand, what can the teacher of emotionally disturbed children use as a buffer for her own mental health?

If a child's behavior is beyond control, exceeding set limits, what does the teacher do when there is no assisting personnel available?

Should an emotionally disturbed child be isolated from, or integrated into, a normal school and/or classroom?

Of what importance do you attribute academic achievement to emotional health?

Questions prepared by Class II for Dr. Sheldon Rappaport:

Discuss the problems of sex in relationship to psychogenically disturbed children.

Without adequate spatial relationships and/or self-concept a child cannot achieve academically. Why?

What responsibility does the classroom teacher assume at Pathway School with regard to each of the therapies?

Under public school budget realities, what are the essential ancillary services?

Discuss pupil's behavior when she is (1) merely adjusting to teacher demands; (2) understanding herself in relation to her problems.

Discuss the teacher's responses when she discovers that classroom misbehavior stems from out-of-school experiences.

When is a child considered too disturbed for public school placement?

What effect do classroom peers have on an individual child in the class for emotionally disturbed children?

COLLATERAL READING

Extensive reading programs were developed for each class. Just as soon as a teacher had been fully accepted into the program and when she was so notified, usually in May prior to September of the year she was to enter the program, she was sent a letter from the project director outlining major details of the experience she was to enter in the fall. At that time she was sent a copy of *A Teaching Method for Brain-Injured and Hyperactive Children* which was to be read prior to the beginning of the fall semester.

Other volumes such as *The Slow Learner in the Classroom* by N. C. Kephart, and *Psychopathology and Education of the Brain-Injured Child* by A. A. Strauss and L. Lehtinen, were brought to the teacher's attention and she was urged to read these also before she arrived at the university.

During the academic year, she was provided with a basic reading list each semester which was to be completed, with reaction reports prepared for each item. Lists of required reading were essentially the same throughout the four years. These are exemplified by those prepared for Class III, noted in the lists below, which accompanied the instructions to the teachers. "It is expected that each of the following will be read by you. A reaction (not an abstract or summary) to the information contained in each is to be prepared and is to be typed on 5" x 8" cards. These will be due no later than January 5. However you may turn them in earlier as you complete them."

The Brain Injured Child, New York Association, pamphlet.

The Brain-Injured Child, Lewis, pamphlet.

The Brain-Injured Child in the Classroom, Kephart, pamphlet.

Discovering Evaluating Programming for the Neurologically Handicapped Child, Strother, pamphlet.

Language Disorders in Children, Wood, pamphlet.

Dallas Medical Journal, pamphlet.

The Other Child, Lewis and Strauss, book.

Success Through Play, Radler and Kephart, book.

Speech and Language Therapy with the Brain Damaged Child, Daley *et al.,* book.

Right-Left Discrimination and Finger Localization, Benton, book.

Psychological Techniques in Neurological Disorders, Burgemeister, book.

An Auditory Approach to Phonics Instruction, Serio and Briggs, book.

"Problems in Conceptualization and Communication in Children with Developmental Alexia," Bender, article.

"Children's Activities for Perceptual Motor Training," Ayers, article.

"The Hazards of Being Born," Barnes, article.

"A Plan for Education," Lehtinen, article.

"Learning Disabilities—An Overview," Bateman, article.

"Implications of Visual Problems in Learning Disability," P. Lewis, article.

"What is the Winter Haven Lion's Story," article.

"Rhythmic Training and Body Balancing Prepare Your Child for Formal Learning," Rice, article.

"Some Principles of Remedial Instruction," Bryant, article.

Psychological Appraisal of Children With Cerebral Defects, Taylor, book.

"Conference on Brain Injury," Strauss and Lehtinen, article.

How To Increase Your Child's Intelligence, Getman, book.

"Specific Reading Disability," Anonymous, article.

Developmental Potential of Preschool Children, Haeusserman, book.

The Montessori Method, Standing, book.

The following reading materials were given to you with the expectation that you would make use of the information in your Tutoring and Motor Training Practicum experience:

Daily Plan Sheet
Behavior Sheet
Vocabulary
A Perceptual Survey Rating Scale, Peterson
Tests for Preference
Physical Performance Test
Strengthening Activities
The Trampoline
A Place to Begin
Physiology of Readiness—P.A.A.S.

A second list follows for which reaction reports were due on May 28th:

"Rhythmic Training and Body Balancing Prepare Your Child for Formal Learning," Rice, article.

The Montessori Method, E. M. Standing, book.

The Montessori Method, Marie Montessori, book.

"Children with Severe Brain Injuries," American Medical Association, article.

"Disabling Myths about Disability," Wright, article.

"Childhood Mental Illness," Littner, article.

When Children Need Special Help with Emotional Problems, Mayer and Hoover, pamphlet.

The Education of Emotionally Handicapped Children, California State Department of Education, pamphlet.

Classes for Emotionally Handicapped, Hollister and Goldstein, pamphlet.

Children of the Evening, Smith, pamphlet.

The Brain-Injured Child, Baldwin, pamphlet.

Problems of Cerebral Dysfunctions, Laufer, pamphlet.

The Brain-Injured Adolescent, Gordon, pamphlet.

How to Increase Your Child's Intelligence, Getman, book.

"Specific Reading Disability," Anonymous, article.

"Conference on Brain Injury," Strauss and Lehtinen, article.

"The Mentally Ill Child in America," F. King, article.

Living with Epileptic Seizures, Livingston, book.

PROJECTS

During the academic year, in relation to the seminar, each student was expected to complete eight major projects which were closely related to both the philosophy and teaching method being described. Again the requirements prepared for Class III are representative of those of the other years. In September the following material pertaining to projects was provided to each student:

The following eight projects are expected to be completed by each Grantee. Four of these projects will be completed during the Fall Semester, and four during the Spring Semester.

The projects will be due in the office no later than 4:00 p.m. on the dates indicated. Each project is expected to:

Reflect the philosophy and methodology presented in the seminars.

Be geared to your anticipated age group next fall.

Consist of a detailed outline for steps in teaching each area.

Demonstrate a representative sample of precise materials to support the outline.

Since you will be working alone next year, we expect that you will prepare your work on an individual basis. Group discussions are excellent, but submitting carbons of outlines and/or materials will not be acceptable.

Fall semester

1. Reading:

Select any one of the following. Involve yourself in an area in which you may expand your present knowledge.

a. Adapt to the philosophy being presented in the seminar (or modify) the project which you will be developing for your present course in Reading (147G).

b. Pursue any one aspect of reading from the point of view being presented. That is:

    (1) Phonics
        (a) Beginning sounds
        (b) Blends
        (c) Digraphs
        (d) Vowels
    (2) Comprehension
    (3) Recall
    (4) Vocabulary
    (5) Game

c. Coordinate and integrate any combination of those listed in (b) above into the seminar philosophy.

2. Visual-Motor-Perception:

a. Develop an original technique which may alleviate and/or compensate for the dysfunction of visual perception in a child.

b. Expand or extend any technique presented in seminar.

3. Self-Concept or Body Image:

Construct a technique using as guidelines the assigned readings, consultants, seminars and other sources which is intended to contribute to the development.

4. Coloring, Cutting and Pasting:

The essentials will be presented to you. Construct representative teaching materials.

DUE: January 22, 1965

Spring semester

Arithmetic:

Details will be presented in seminar. Much of the material will be constructed during our sessions. Each is expected to construct *one* technique in addition to class prepared material by either expanding, extending or filling in a gap.

Writing:

This outline will be presented in seminar. Each teacher is expected to construct a representative sampling of the teaching materials. You will also be expected to construct one addition to this material by either expanding, extending or filling in a gap.

Language development:

Develop a technique using as guidelines the assigned readings, consultants, your tutoring/teaching experience and other sources.

Visual-Motor-Perception:

a. Develop an extension to your Fall Project, or

b. Construct a new project using as guidelines the assigned readings, consultants, and/or your tutoring/teaching experience.

DUE: May 30, 1965

PREPARATION OF PRE-ACADEMIC MATERIALS

In order to be assured that the teachers were thoroughly familiar with the preparation and construction of basic readiness materials which involved visuo-motor perception, several sessions of the seminar during the spring term were devoted to the construction of different types of items. In this way each teacher would have available a library of models which could be used the following year. Many other models were provided for the teacher, but essential elements included the following, together with instructions to the teachers of Class III:

The following teaching materials will be presented in detail and constructed in part during our sessions. It is expected that each of you will complete these materials, organize and code them for your future use. These teaching materials should form a basis for educational programming for each child in your next year's class.

Peg designs:
One design from each of the developmental levels.

Block designs:
One design from each developmental level.

Mosaic designs:
A sampling of patterns to serve as a future source of information.

Parquetry designs:
A sampling of patterns to serve as a future source of information.

Puzzles:
Several puzzles demonstrating the sequence for cutting and levels of difficulty.

Coding:
Organized to show sequence of development.

Copying geometric forms:
Organized to show sequence of development.

DUE: May 21, 1965

ACTIVITIES RELATED DIRECTLY TO CHILDREN

As an integral part of the seminar the teachers-in-training were obligated to spend a great deal of time each week with brain-injured and hyperactive children in activities of a widely diversified nature.

In order that the teachers might see the reasons for the many examinations which were being recommended for brain-injured children as a part of the seminar theory material, each child in the demonstration class was annually given an extensive series of examinations of a multidisciplinary nature. Two or three teachers were assigned to *observe each of the examinations on each child,* hence the teachers witnessed the pediatric examination to ascertain the general health picture of the child. They observed an extensive psychological examination of the child during which a wide variety of equipment was utilized—equipment which was being mentioned almost daily in the seminar sessions; they accompanied the child to the hospital and observed the making of an electroencephalogram and its reading; they observed psychiatric, ophthalmological, speech and auditory examinations, as well as an occasional optometric examination. They were given an opportunity to see what values each examination had for a greater understanding of the child in the educational program, and could also observe the limitations of certain professional evaluations for educational practice. The teachers, in addition to the professional reports submitted by the various specialists, prepared their own reports of their observations of the child during the examination situation. These were essentially behavioral observations, not clinical evaluations.

Each teacher-in-training was assigned a child in the demonstration class for observational purposes. From a separate observation room or from closed-circuit television, the teacher was required to observe the child for one hour each day, four days a week, for the academic year and to prepare a written report on each observation. The observations were scheduled so that, over a period of time, the teacher observed the child at different times during the school day, thus being able to see the child perform under conditions of fatigue as well as when he was refreshed. These observations involved a large time segment for the teachers, and over the years they became an important source of information regarding the educational growth of the child. They became invaluable aids in helping to determine when a child was ready for return to the regular class in his neighborhood school.

Each day teachers, usually in pairs, accompanied one child on an informal walk outside the school building for about twenty-minutes. The walks were customarily preplanned, but in every instance they were carried out within the educational frame of reference which was being advocated. In this way the teachers could get to know the child that they were observing in the demonstration class on an informal basis.

The reader will understand the nature and depth of the observational experience by examining carefully the following instructions to the teachers, observation schedules, and report forms.

1. Instructions for reporting observations:

a. A schedule has been made. Please adhere to it unless an extreme emergency arises (see attached schedule).

b. Reports are to be typed and are due within 24 hours following the specific observation.

c. Reports will be expected to include the following in order to observe change in behavior throughout the year.

> (1) Specific anecdotal records of the child.
> (2) Academic work and overt behavior reaction of the child.
> (3) Factual information—nothing judicial:
>> (a) Is the work checked before it is put away?
>> (b) Are errors corrected immediately or later?
> (4) Objective record of what you see and hear:
>> (a) Response of child to directions given by teacher or assistant.
>> (b) Response of teacher to child.
> (5) Information that will help us develop a better educational program for the child. We are interested to find:
>> (a) Is there a pattern to a type of behavior?
>> (b) Are there times when the child demonstrates this behavior and times when he doesn't?

d. See attached sheet for Observation formats.

Each observation schedule lasted for approximately a two-week period, and was changed thereafter from time to time to insure that each teacher was able not only to observe the child at different times during the day and in different activities but also to make room for different types of teacher-child activities, i.e., the inclusion of tutorial activities as the teachers became prepared to handle them.

As noted earlier, each teacher was to provide a report of each observation within 24 hours of the time of observing. This time limitation was imposed in order that observed behavior could be reported while it was immediately in the minds of the observer and in order that one day's behavior would not be confused with that of another day. The format suggested below was employed by the teachers for recording any contact which they had with the child during which behavioral observations could be made:

Observation Formats

Date

1. To be used *now* and until further assignments. To be used when your assigned child is absent from classroom.

Observation—General

Date   Teacher's Name
Time

2. For reporting the observation of your *assigned* child.

Observation

Child's Name   Teacher's Name
Date
Time

3. For reporting your assigned days in the room.

Observation—Walk

Child's Name   Teacher's Name
Date
Time

Observation—Lunch and Rest

Date   Teacher's Name
Time

4. For reporting Motor Training.

Observation—Motor Training

Child's Name   Teacher's Name

Dates

Time

Test:

Teach:

Review:

Comments:

   Test:

   Teach:

   Review:

General Comments:

During the last three years of the project the teachers worked in pairs in a motor training program for thirty minutes four days per week. This was definitely an extension of the classroom program, and it was carried on in ways intended to support the learning activities of the child in the classroom. The basic program followed in this phase of the experience was that advocated by Getman [8] and by Kephart [9].

In the first year, an attempt was made to provide a practice-teaching experience for each teacher in the group of brain-injured children. This had to be stopped, because it was observed that the children were not able to tolerate the large number of adults in the classroom each day entailed by the practice-teaching. From time to time, individual teachers were assigned responsibilities with the children as assistants during the lunch experience, during an informal but controlled recreation period, during rest periods, or in other ways, but this was not done consistently with all twelve teachers all of the time each year.

During the last three years, teachers singly or in pairs, carried on daily tutorial lessons with individual children to substitute for the practice-teaching activities. During these periods, which generally lasted for sixty minutes four days a week, the teachers emphasized pre-academic training for the most part. Skill-building in reading and number concepts, and the pre-academic and readiness activities essential to these concepts, were stressed. Teachers had an opportunity to try out teaching materials which had been made by them as a part of the seminar experience and to ascertain what was appropriate and what was not.

All of these seemingly separate activities on the part of the teachers were obviously related back to the formal sessions of the seminar, and an opportunity for informal discussion of them was available there. In this respect another, but unplanned, element should be mentioned. While all of the activities related to the seminar, including the demonstration class, were carried on in the same building, students needed a place to work when they were actually constructing materials. Initially, they turned the office of one of the faculty members into an informal meeting place until this made serious inroads on faculty time and activity. By then, the importance of this type of facility was recognized and a room adjoining the faculty office was made available on an almost full-time basis for teacher use. Here teachers could meet to talk, to work together on projects, to discuss children, and to talk informally with faculty members. The staff conferences were also held in this room. This informal sharing of ideas and small-group work became a very important element in the total preparation program. The faculty also became aware that, on an unplanned basis, teachers were meeting in night sessions on a regular schedule, the purpose of which was the pooling of information gained from reading and other sources. This technique was used especially when students were over-loaded and when, as a stopgap measure, responsibilities for covering the total problem could be parceled out to individuals and then shared with the whole group. While these techniques were not required by the faculty members involved, they may have indeed been necessary from the point of view of the teachers, in the face of the heavy demands which were made on their available time.

During the fourth year of the program, the year in which the training phase terminated, plans had to be made for the children of the demonstration class who would need special assistance for additional years ahead. As children in the demonstration group who no longer needed the special class were transferred back to their regular neighborhood schools they were not replaced by new children. The demonstration class was thus reduced to an exceedingly small group of children during the last three or four months of the fourth year. It was actually too small to provide adequate experiences for the members of Class IV. To compensate for this, plans were made in cooperation with public school systems in and around Syracuse, New York, for the teachers of Class IV to work in the schools on a tutorial basis with children who had been identified as being hyperactive and brain-injured. This tutorial experience, different for this group from that of the members of Classes I, II, and III, was carried on for most of the school year for sixty minutes four times a week. In this way, the teachers could obtain some direct experience with these children and could have an opportunity to test teaching materials which had been developed for them in terms of the specific psychopathology which was presented.

The Tutoring—Observation form utilized by the teachers in reporting both their observations and their activities during tutoring experiences regardless of whether these activities involved motor training, academic emphases with reading or number concepts, or visuomotor training is presented on page 52.

STAFF MEETING

As an ancillary activity to the seminar, staff conferences were held periodically. These were concerned with the children in the demonstration class. One session a month of this nature was scheduled, each lasting for approximately three hours, and one child was considered at each staff conference. These conferences were attended by all teachers as observers. Participating in the staff conference were the project director, psychologists, social workers, the demonstration teacher, and the faculty member responsible for the methods and materials phase of the seminar. In addition, under the supervision of the latter, one or two teachers were responsible for the presentation of material resulting from

TUTORING—OBSERVATION

Child_____Date_____Trainees_____

MOTOR TRAINING   READING—ARITHMETIC

Materials

_____

APPROACH
Positive (+)
Negative (—)

_____

ACHIEVEMENT
Strengths

_____

ACHIEVEMENT
Weaknesses

_____

Comments

VISUAL PERCEPTUAL TRAINING   OTHER

Materials

_____

APPROACH
Positive (+)
Negative (—)

_____

ACHIEVEMENT
Strengths

_____

ACHIEVEMENT
Weaknesses

_____

Comments

motor training activities, tutorial sessions, or recent educational evaluations which might have been made with the child being considered. The teachers-in-training were thus able to observe the workings of a multidisciplinary staff and were able to see the development of logical recommendations being made regarding the child's progress, his relationship with the school, the need for ancillary psychotherapy, parental counseling, or further examinations to facilitate a better understanding of his problems.

PARTICIPATION IN THE ADMINISTRATORS' SEMINAR

While teacher activities related to their seminar are being discussed, it should also be mentioned that during the period of the administrators' seminar, the teachers attended all these sessions as well. During this period, all other teacher activities were suspended except attendance at university courses.

It can be seen that the demands on the teachers were many, and that a tremendous amount of learning went on in informal, but planned ways outside of university courses. A reference room located in the same building as all of the other activities related to the seminar was available for teacher use. Because time was of the essence, attempts were made to have available multiple copies of all basic materials which the teachers were asked to read. A dozen copies of almost every major reference work were placed in the reference room, and these could be checked out to the teachers for extended periods of time. There was little problem, therefore, regarding access to the reading material. In intensive programs such as the one being described here, the availability of reading materials is an essential element. Funds were allocated which permitted the purchase of any book, pamphlet, microfilm, or reprint relating to the program desired by either university faculty or a teacher-in-training. While this service extended over the four-year period, extensive resources were available beginning with Class I. In addition to the reference room resources, the basic texts and numerous pamphlet materials which might be required for the following year were purchased and given to the teachers to become a part of their personal libraries.

RELATED COURSES PERTAINING TO EMOTIONALLY DISTURBED
CHILDREN

It was mentioned in the list of university courses basic to the
masters degree program that a two-semester course dealing with
the education of emotionally disturbed children was incorporated
as a significant part of the sequence for each teacher. This part was
under the supervision of Peter Knoblock, Ph.D., Associate Professor, Syracuse University. Dr. Knoblock taught one-half of this program with a second faculty member, who was sometimes responsible
for the other half. Although somewhat different emphases were
made in this course from that stressed by Dr. Cruickshank in his
part of the major seminar, the two together were believed to provide
a broad background of understanding of the total field for each
teacher. Psychopathology, classroom materials based upon psychopathology, an understanding of the dynamics of group and individual behavior, the impact of tension on adjustment and learning,
and basic concepts pertaining to the theory of personality and
learning disorders were gained from one or another source. The
university faculty was alert to reports of overlapping in order that
steps could be taken to minimize this. In actual fact, however,
very little, if any, overlapping occurred between the two types of
presentations. It should also be added that Dr. Knoblock served
in a consultant capacity throughout the four years, attended all
staff conferences, supervised the psychological personnel in the
project, and performed other valuable services to the teachers-in-
training.

FIELD EXPERIENCES

Few field experiences were provided to the teachers. This was
both because of the limitations in teacher time and because of the
limited values which are accrued from short observational visits.
Class I made a visit of several days to the Pathway School, a
residential and day school, one division of which was devoted solely
to the education of brain-injured and hyperactive children at that
time. Class III attended the professional meetings of the Council
for Exceptional Children at its international meeting in Toronto,

Canada, and participated in discussions pertinent to this phase of special education. Students in Classes III and IV each participated in an annual two-day conference on the education of emotionally disturbed children held annually at Syracuse University, and they were provided with the complete proceedings of these meetings. Students in Classes II, III, and IV also participated in a one-day conference on organic problems of speech held at Syracuse University. Other group field experiences had been discussed by the project faculty and had been rejected as required group activities because of the inordinate amount of time which the teachers had to devote to the project. Many students made individual field trips which were related to the program, but these were not uniform among all teachers and are not considered a part of the present report.

The Administrators' Seminar

Reference has been made to the administrators' seminar and the reason for including this in the project program. Educational programs fail in pubilc schools so often because of a failure to achieve good understanding between teachers and administrators regarding the project that definite steps were taken to try to avoid this impasse with this program. If the reader will refer himself to the collateral reference to this project report (Cf., Cruickshank, *The Brain-Injured Child in Home, School, and Community, op. cit.*) or to other writings noted at the end of this chapter, he will observe the complexity in the educational program for these children and the numerous ways in which it differs from general elementary education practice [10, 11]. It was obvious that without a great deal of orientation there would be many points on which misunderstanding could occur between teachers and principals. This, the authors felt, could not be permitted to become the basis for lack of program success. Neither could it be assumed that in a short, but intensive, period of seven days a full understanding of the problem could be accomplished. However, it was felt that major strides toward complete understanding could be accomplished and that this would go far to insure appropriate results from the program of teacher preparation.

Since the time the administrators were to spend at the university was limited, reading materials were provided prior to the beginning of the seminar. As soon as the name of the administrator was known, letters were sent to him indicating the nature of the program he would be attending. Considerable orientation could be provided through correspondence which would create a mental set on the part of each administrator and provide a basis for immediate action once the group assembled. Requests regarding reading were made at this time. Each administrator was provided a copy of the basic text being used by the teachers, and he was expected to have read this prior to his arrival at the University. He was also expected to have made himself familiar with the books on the following reading list, which could be obtained from his own school professional library or from nearby university libraries:

Success Through Play, Radler and Kephart (1960), Harper and Row, New York and Evanston.

The Other Child, Lewis and Strauss (1951), Grune and Stratton, 381 Fourth Avenue, New York, New York.

Psychopathology and Education of the Brain-Injured Child, Vol. I, Strauss and Lehtinen (1947), Grune and Stratton, 381 Fourth Avenue, New York, New York.

Psychopathology and Education of the Brain-Injured Child, Vol. II, Strauss and Kephart (1955), Grune and Stratton, 381 Fourth Avenue, New York, New York.

The Slow Learner in the Classroom, Kephart (1960), Charles E. Merrill, Inc., Columbus, Ohio.

Right-Left Discrimination and Finger Localization, Benton, A. L. (1959), Hoeber-Harper Book, Harper Brothers, 49 East 33rd Street, New York 16, New York.

Psychological Appraisals of Children with Cerebral Defects, Taylor (1959), The Commonwealth Fund, Harvard University Press, Cambridge, Massachusetts.

Living with Epileptic Seizures, Livingston (1963), Charles C Thomas, Publisher, Springfield, Illinois.

Developmental Potential of Preschool Children, Else Haeussermann (1958), Grune and Stratton, 381 Fourth Avenue, New York, New York.

The Montessori Method, E. M. Standing (1962), The Academy Library Guild, Box 549, Fresno, California.

How to Increase your Child's Intelligence, Getman, G. N., O. D. (1962), Luverne, Minnesota.

Brain Damage in Children, The Biological and Social Aspects, H. Birch, ed. (1964), Williams and Wilkins Co., Baltimore, Maryland.

Childhood Aphasia (1962), California Society for Crippled Children and Adults, 251 Kearny Street, San Francisco, California.

The Aphasic Child, Hortense Barry (1961), The Volta Bureau, Washington, D.C.

The Treatment and Prevention of Reading Problems, Carl H. Delacato (1959), Charles C Thomas, Springfield, Illinois.

Childhood Aphasia and Brain Damage—A Definition, Sheldon R. Rappaport (ed.), Vol. I (1964), Pathway School, Box 181, Norristown, Pa., 19404

Aphasic Children, Mildred A. McGinnis (1963), Volta Bureau, Washington, D.C.

It was ascertained that, for the most part, each administrator approached the pre-seminar reading assignments seriously and had really done what was requested of him. With this background of information, immediate attention could be given to the details of the program within the time limitation of the seminar itself. Each administrator was provided on arrival with four or five additional volumes, from which he was either to read designated portions or to scan in entirety during the time he was at the university. These volumes included:

F. Redl and D. Wineman, *The Aggressive Child;* F. Redl, *Mental Hygiene in the Classroom;* N. Haring and L. Phillips, *Educating Emotionally Disturbed Children;* A. A. Strauss and E. Lehtinen, *Psychopathology and Education of the Brain Injured Child;* Radler and N. C. Kephart, *Success Through Play.*

The university personnel took much care in planning for the seminar. These seminars remained the same in their basic form during the four years of the teacher education program. Members of the seminar assembled in Syracuse, usually during the month of May, after the major portion of the preparation program for the teachers had been completed. They arrived in time to attend a first session on Sunday afternoon and they remained in attendance through the following Saturday. During this period of time two types of activities were planned: those in which administrators would meet individually with project personnel, and those in which they would meet as a group.

1.   The mornings were devoted to five different types of activities. Eight clock hours of time were set aside during the period of the seminar for each administrator and his teacher for the purpose of local planning. This permitted them to work together on the details of program organization which would be required in order to initiate the class the following fall. This also proved to be a time when the administrator could get to know his future teacher, understand her professional goals, and her ways of achieving them. It was a time when, without interruption from any other source, the administrator could devote a major amount of his attention to the nature of the program, the physical modifications which would have to be made to the classroom, the needed supplies, the organization of volunteer groups, the screening of children, and a variety of other problems which would require discussion with the superintendent of schools or his representative upon his return to the school system.

Four clock-hours were devoted to periods when the administrator could observe the demonstration class of hyperactive and brain-injured children. These were scheduled at different hours during the morning throughout the school week so that the administrators could observe the children under different conditions and in different types of learning activities. The teacher usually accompanied the administrator to the observations, for by that time in the academic year, most of the teachers could serve as excellent translators of the program to their administrators.

In addition to the above, one hour during the week was provided so that the individual administrator, alone or with his teacher, could talk informally with the project director about specific questions which were pertinent only to the school district from which they came and to which they would return. Two clock-hours were spent by the administrator with Miss Ruth Cheves, who had previously prepared suggested lists of equipment and materials which would be required for the following year. (The time spent in these conferences usually pertained solely to materials, their nature, and their use.) Finally, one hour was planned for each administrator to spend with the project psychologist in discussing specific aspects of the psychodiagnostic program as these might relate to the school district he represented. In all, sixteen clock-hours of conferences and observation were incorporated in the schedule of each administrator during five days of the seminar week.

2. The afternoons and some evenings were devoted to group meetings and discussions which were attended by all administrators and teachers-in-training. It was during these sessions that the staff attempted to encapsulate for the administrators most of what the teachers had experienced during the preceding several months of their training. Since both teachers and administrators now heard the same discussion, these sessions served as a point of future reference for both groups. These sessions usually lasted for approximately three hours. A typical schedule of topics in any one year included the following:

Sunday	Learning theory basic to the program.
Monday	Continuation of the above; essential elements of program.
Tuesday P.M.	Visuomotor training.
Tuesday Eve.	Continuation of above.
Wednesday	Pupil selection, admission, separation, pupil transportation.
Thursday	Psychological services needed to support program.
Friday	Educational planning, teaching methodology, ordering materials, teacher preparation.
Friday Eve.	The diagnostic team and utilization of ancillary personnel.
Saturday A.M.	Classroom modifications; role of the teacher in the program (admission, separation); ancillary personnel and their relationship to the teacher and children; use of volunteers.
P.M. Session	Relationship of local program to the university research follow-up program.

It can be seen from the above, and from the description of the morning activities which were scheduled during the administrators' seminar, that by the end of the seminar the administrators had at least been exposed to the major problems which might be faced by a teacher and by a school principal in the course of the initial development of the program. The extent to which this phase of the project accomplished what was intended will be reported in later chapters of this monograph.

In a few instances, superintendents of schools approached the project director for guidance in the selection of the school principal under whom the program would develop, and sought guidelines from the university for principal-selection somewhat similar to those provided in the selection of the teachers. As much assistance as could be given was provided, usually by telephone. This, however, was not uniform in any degree, and the project personnel usually had nothing to do with the selection of the principal who attended the seminar.

THE DEMONSTRATION CLASS

The demonstration class served as a focal point around which much of the discussions in the seminar and staff conferences were oriented. This class was organized within the university classroom building in which most aspects of the teacher preparation program and administrators' seminar were centered. In cooperation with the Syracuse Public Schools, this class was designated as an integral part of the special education program of that school system.

During the first year of the project, the demonstration teacher was fully employed by the University and was in no way related to the school district. The same individual also conducted the seminar on teacher method. This proved to be an extraordinarily poor decision on the part of the project director, for it failed to take into consideration the tremendous amount of time which was required by the demonstration phase of the program. As soon as the situation was understood, the responsibilities of demonstration and college teaching were divided, and during the remaining three years two persons filled these separate positions. The teacher of the demonstration class during the last three years of the project was an employee of the school district and was paid by the district. The children included in the class were recruited from schools in the same district. The teacher was paid her salary from the district and thus maintained retirement, health insurance, and other benefits without interruption. The university reimbursed the salary in full to the district; the district contributed the cost of fringe benefits. The director of special education of the district served as the liaison person between the project director in the university and the many aspects of the program in the school district which were ultimately involved.

When this division of seminar-demonstration responsibility took place, the university faculty member was then available to spend his full time with the teachers-in-training. During the first half of each training year this person spent a great deal of time with the teachers in the observation room, and attempted to relate theoretical comments and methodological procedures which were being stressed in the formal meetings of the seminar with observed behavior of the children in the demonstration class.

THE CHILDREN

The maximum number of children included in the demonstration class was eight. This arbitrary teacher-pupil ratio was determined on the basis of previous experience by the project director in developing classes for brain-injured and hyperactive children in other parts of the country and during the Syracuse-Montgomery project, where the teacher-pupil ratio had been one-to-ten. This had proved to be too large a load for maximal supervision by a good teacher and an assistant. Experience in numerous situations supported the one-to-eight relationship, but even this proved to be too high on many occasions, and reductions in the size of the group often took place.

The children were all boys between the ages of seven and thirteen. All were at least nine years old on admission to the demonstration class, but during the latter three years the admission age was held at seven. Girls were not excluded, but during the four years of the program no girls were referred although requests had been made for their inclusion. It has been pointed out elsewhere that the ratio of boys to girls within the affected group is much in favor of males, but it is unusual that in this period of time no girls were referred by the schools.

In general, all of the boys were of normal intelligence. In only one instance was a mentally retarded child included, and this was done in order to demonstrate to the teachers the applicability of the procedures to this clinical problem. When the child no longer required the specialized training of this class, however, he was returned to a special education program for mentally handicapped children in his own school district and he was not replaced by another retarded child. Intelligence quotients varied within the group from those which would normally be classified in the slow learner or dull normal group to several in the high normal and superior levels.

Initially, all referrals were made following an extensive series of conferences with school psychologists, school social workers, and special education personnel, during which time an attempt was made to provide them with a thorough understanding of the type of child being sought. This understanding improved over the four-year period, and more and more homogeneous groups of brain-injured and hyperactive children with common characteristics of psychopathology were obtained, though this was far from the case at first, and it illustrates a problem which all new programs are likely to encounter.

In spite of attempts to obtain a meeting of minds among professional personnel responsible for screening and referral, people do act as individuals and they approach the problem from their own perspectives and orientations. This can result in a disastrous situation from the point of view of effective classroom programs, as almost happened in the case of the project demonstration class. While the experience provided a unique opportunity for teachers to observe the problems resulting from poor selection and admission procedures, the results were disastrous both for the children and the demonstration teacher.

The significance of a good admissions program cannot be overstressed. Once a child is admitted to the program and is included in the group, it may take several months for the teacher to thoroughly understand the nature of his behavior, therefore an adequate basis is needed for requesting his exclusion, if exclusion seems warranted. If undue delay occurs, both the teacher and other children have wasted a great deal of valuable time. This was the case in the demonstration class provided for Class I. Lack of understanding of the nature of the desired children on the part of admissions personnel resulted in inclusion of some children in the program who were not only hyperactive and/or brain-injured, but in several instances were prepsychotic. The depth of these children's problems required long-term and constant psychotherapy as well as educational supports. The public school program is rarely assumed to be adequate to meet the needs of this group of children. Certainly the philosophy of teacher preparation and of education of brain-injured and hyperactive children, as espoused by these authors, recognizes limitations in the abilities of the best teachers and limitations in the range of problems in children which even outstanding teachers may be expected to cope with effectively. Once again it is emphasized that optimal teaching is based upon optimal conditions of homogeneity. These are certainly possible in a large school system.

As soon as the above-mentioned problem was understood by the program administrators, immediate decisions were made to exclude certain children, either permanently or temporarily, who failed to meet the diagnostic criteria for the class. The group was restructured, and children were added who did meet the criteria and who were capable of responding to instruction. During the second half of the first academic year, however, the demonstration class was reduced from eight to four. This number was gradually increased, but it never rose to eight again that year. In subsequent years the teacher-pupil ratio was one-to-eight for the most part. Daily fluctuations were experienced, of course, and from time to time a given child would be temporarily excluded for a period of a few days when this action appeared to be in his interest.

RATIONALE

The classroom used for the demonstration program was not an ideal room situation, but it came close to achieving the desired characteristics. The room modification, as well as the teaching

Figure 1.   Nonstimulating classroom used for purposes of demonstration during teacher preparation program. Reproduced with permission from W. M. Cruickshank, *The Brain-Injured Child in Home, School, and Community* (Syracuse: Syracuse University Press, 1967).

method to be employed, followed closely the methodology and point of view which was stressed with the teachers in the seminar. It followed the modifications of the Strauss-Lehtinen concepts which have been advocated by Cruickshank in previous writings [12, 13, 14]. Specifically, as noted in Figures 1 and 2, this included a marked reduction in extraneous environmental stimuli in the room. Unessential visual and auditory stimuli were removed from the learning area, or were reduced as far as possible to a point where their influence on learning would be negligible. In Figure 1 it can be observed that transparent window lights were replaced with opaque glass. Fluorescent lighting fixtures were replaced with incandescent fixtures, since the former often produce a humming sound and sometimes flicker. The walls, furniture, and other elements of the room were painted the same color to reduce visual stimuli. The ceiling was sound treated and the floor was covered with a wall-to-wall carpet to further reduce internally created auditory stimuli. Figure 2 illustrates the cupboard arrangement within

Figure 2. A second view of nonstimulating classroom used in conjunction with teacher preparation program. Reproduced with permission from W. M. Cruickshank, *The Brain-Injured Child in Home, School, and Community* (Syracuse: Syracuse University Press, 1967).

the room, i.e., each shelf was enclosed with wooden doors so that the children would not be visually distracted by the different colored and shaped materials which might be stored there. The classroom was self-contained. The door noted in Figure 2 leads to an adjoining toilet room. This obviated the necessity for the children to pass along stimulating corridors and encounter other people in the routine of getting to and from their room and toilet facilities. The self-contained nature of the classroom thus reduced the level of stimuli to which the children were exposed.

In keeping with the theoretical model which was advocated, there was also a concern to reduce space. The reduction of space further reduces stimuli, and also provides a spatial area in which a child can experience easier adjustment. While room size has never been made a matter of definitive investigation, the room depicted in Figures 1 and 2 measured 14′ x 22′; considerably smaller than a standard classroom. Furthermore, as the figures indicate, each child was provided with a personal cubicle in which the great majority of his learning experience took place, which served also to further reduce the spatial area involved in his adjustment.

Other variables which were inherent in the teaching model and which were consistently utilized in the demonstration program involved: (a) the structuring of all aspects of the individual and group activities of the daily program; and (b) the development of a wide assortment of special teaching materials. The latter were developed specific to each child. They reflected and were dependent on the psychopathology which had been demonstrated by the child in the various psychological, psychiatric, or educational examinations. During the continuous evaluation of the children, and as changes in psychopathology were observed, these were reflected in changes in the nature of the teaching materials which were utilized.

Programs of individual motor training and tutorial experiences, which have been described in an earlier section of this chapter, completed the daily program for the children. There was little in the demonstration program which was atypical of that which would be possible in a public school system except for the tutoring program. This was essential for the teacher-preparation phase of the program, and might be an aspect of the program which could not be duplicated conveniently in the average school. However, the teachers-in-training were exposed to the ways in which volunteers could be used in the motor training aspect of the program, and these concepts could be utilized in tutorial extensions of a school program if it were deemed appropriate.

It must not be assumed that the demonstration class was a perfect model educational program. It approximated a model, but there were many things which minimized its model qualities. First, the presence of twelve teachers-in-training each year meant that the children in the demonstration class were required to adjust to an unusually large number of adults. When to these adults were added the teacher, the aide, the social workers, the psychologist, the university faculty personnel, and others, it is easy to see that a model for exact duplication was not utilized. Furthermore, during the first year, when the demonstration teacher was also responsible for the phase of the seminar involving methods of teaching and teaching materials, a common point of view was achieved between theory and practice. During the latter three years, when these functions became the responsibility of two persons, there was often a gulf between advocated and practiced method. The normal problems of individual difference in point of view, or in interpretation of the point of view, resulted in variations between theory and practice which were often obvious. Rather than being a negative characteristic, these differences often made it possible to illustrate behavioral reactions and learning problems which otherwise would have been impossible. The concepts of the model were distorted to this degree, however.

DEMONSTRATION CLASS PERSONNEL

Personnel who served in the demonstration class or with the children and who were utilized as members of the model being advocated included the following.

1. The *demonstration teacher* has already been mentioned. Although two teachers were utilized at different times, as has been indicated, both were persons of long experience with children. Both held masters degrees and both had taught exceptional children for many years previous to their appointment as demonstration teachers. When it became apparent that it would be necessary to separate demonstration teaching from seminar participation, a demonstration teacher who had been a member of Class I was sought in order to maintain consistency in point of view, both for the children and for the teachers, in the three classes which would follow.

The demonstration teacher, of course, played a significant role both with the children and with the teachers-in-training. Cruickshank has advocated that the teacher of brain-injured and hyperactive children must play an important role in many key decisions regarding the educational plan for the children. The demonstration teacher was therefore primarily responsible for decisions regarding the time of admission of the child to the class, occasions when the child should be temporarily excluded from the class, and recommendations regarding the time when the child should be considered for return to his regular assignment in his neighborhood school. Teachers-in-training thus were able to observe the functioning of the demonstration teacher in these important areas of decision.

The demonstration teacher likewise met periodically with the parents in an evaluation of the progress and status of each child in the various aspects of the educational program. Teachers-in-training often observed these parent conferences, which in large part substituted for a report card. The conferences were supplemental to a written statement of the child's progress which had been prepared by the teacher and given to the parents prior to the conference.

The demonstration teacher was also an important member of the staff conferences. When decisions were made to return the child to the regular school program, the demonstration teacher was the one to whom the responsibility was assigned for giving the new receiving teacher a complete insight into the educational status of the child. At other levels, the project director worked with the receiving principal, the social worker, and the visiting teacher assigned to the receiving school.

This teacher also participated in the seminars with the teachers-in-training from time to time, and provided them with a logical basis for their understanding of certain teacher-pupil relationships which had been observed. Teachers-in-training frequently sought out the demonstration teacher for informal conversations aimed at greater understanding of the reasons for demonstration class activities or decisions. Informal contacts of this nature took place almost continuously throughout the academic year.

2. The *teacher assistant,* long advocated by the project director as a basic element in any program for hyperactive and brain-injured children, was utilized in the demonstration class. Four different assistants were used during the four years: two for a few months each, one for one year, and the fourth for two years. Changes of personnel in this position were due in two cases to personality factors which could not be tolerated, and to the fact that the third assistant had to move from the community. The frequent changes were not good insofar as the program for the children was concerned but, on the other hand, the situation provided a remarkable laboratory experience for the teachers-in-training and demonstrated, at least for Classes I and II, the necessity for careful preliminary appraisal of personality characteristics of the assistant. The teachers saw that pre-employment recommendations, interviews, and administrative decisions which had taken place do not always result in obtaining qualified assistants, so the change of

personnel involved in this position was not considered a negative factor from the point of view of training. During the course of the latter three years, outstanding non-professional assistants were obtained and these were able to demonstrate a remarkable model for the teacher observers.

3. The *project psychiatrist* performed two functions. The first has already been described, namely, the instructional function with the teachers in the seminar. Second, however, he also provided psychiatric consultation to the demonstration teacher. It has long been the considered opinion of the senior author that the best teachers of brain-injured and hyperactive children require added personal supports in order to maintain themselves at a high functional level. Good teachers often internalize the problems of their children, and teaching effectiveness is likely to decline if problem internalization continues uninterrupted for too long. Therefore two periods per month were incorporated in the teacher's schedule where she received psychiatric consultation for two hours each time. During these periods, which were unrecorded, the teacher and psychiatrist could cover any area they desired. Some preliminary structure was provided to the teacher and to the psychiatrist during which it was emphasized that the goal of this consultation was to assist the teacher in better understanding the behavior dynamics of the children in her class and her relationships to them. However, it was stressed that the conversations could depart from these areas as far as was desired by both teacher and psychiatrist. These sessions were never observed by the teachers-in-training, and the content of the conversations was not divulged at any later time. The teachers-in-training did, however, become aware of the significance of this educational technique and, in various ways, were able to assess its importance to their own future professional behavior.

4. *Social work trainees,* working under supervision, were always mature persons with extensive earlier experience with emotionally disturbed children. Each of these persons served in the capacity of a school social worker and functioned in a number of diverse and important ways. Through their performance, teachers were able to become aware of the vital and important roles which school social workers can play in an educational program for brain-injured and hyperactive children. The social workers developed pre-

admission social case histories of children being considered for admission; they served as the liaison persons between the demonstration class, the teacher, the home, community agencies, and the school system; they carried on parent-counseling sessions and discussion sessions for separate groups of fathers and mothers; they presented basic data regarding the child and his familial situation in the class staff conferences, and each served as secretary for conferences. In these and other ways, the teachers became aware of the role which the social worker can and must play in any optimal program of education.

5. The *project director* played several roles with respect to the demonstration class and these varied in intensity from week to week and from year to year. Since the demonstration class was located in a university building, the teacher had no school building principal with whom to relate. The project director filled this role. He also—both in his capacity as pseudo-principal and as a psychologist—served as a crisis teacher when this was needed. He often handled the Life Space Interview and the restructuring which might be necessary for readmission of a child to the demonstration class as a participating member.

He served to reduce obvious differences in procedures between the demonstration teacher and the faculty members who were responsible for methods and materials in the seminar, or to interpret the reasons for these differences if reduction could not be effected. He served as chairman for most of the staff conferences. If administrative decisions were ultimately required and could not be achieved by consensus, he made these decisions. Some of these roles were observed by the teachers-in-training; others, appropriately, were not. Teachers were invited to observe the Life Space Interview, for example. Crises do not always conveniently take place when observers are present, however, so most of these opportunities for direct observation could not be utilized by the teachers. The project director also attempted to keep constantly informed on all matters concerning the project. In this fashion, during the seminar periods for which he had a direct responsibility, an integration of concepts and a synthesis of ideas and activities could be effected.

6. The *psychologist* served the demonstration class by provid-

ing continuous evaluation of the children, by interpreting data from these examinations to the demonstration teacher and informally to the teachers-in-training, and by presenting the psychological data during the staff conferences. On some occasions the psychologist also worked directly with parents, although this was usually the responsibility of the social worker.

7. A *graduate assistant* to the project director also often worked directly with the demonstration teacher. Sometimes this was in the role of an assistant, sometimes as a crisis teacher, sometimes as an interpreter between teacher and project director, and most often as an expediter of one aspect or another of the complicated program.

8. Previous mention has been made of the role which Miss Ruth Cheves played with Classes II, III, and IV in connection with the demonstration class. As the person responsible for methods and materials, Miss Cheves sat with the teachers-in-training in the observation room for many weeks each year, watching the demonstration class, interpreting children's behavior, carrying on a running critique of teacher and assistant behavior, and answering questions which were raised by the observers. She knew each of the children in the demonstration class very well, and thus she was in a unique position to match child and teaching situation for the teachers as they were becoming acquainted with the children and the program.

POST-TRAINING EVALUATION

A post-training evaluation was planned as a part of the project, and personnel were added to the project staff toward the end of the first year to begin this phase of the evaluation. Three persons were responsible for this during the five-year project: one for one year, and two each for two years. All of these persons had faculty status, were mature and experienced educators, and had a thorough orientation to the theoretical framework of the project. While these persons had little contact with the teachers-in-training during the academic year (they were performing site visits during most of this time), time was provided so that evaluators and teachers-in-training could get to know one another.

Following the termination of the training year, the evaluators visited each class and teacher in her own school district every year during the remaining years of the project. Members of Class I were visited in each of four years subsequent to their training year; Class II members, for three years; Class III, for two years; and Class IV, for one year. The nature of the evaluation program will be discussed in Chapter III.

REFERENCES

1. Throughout this report all teachers will be referred to as feminine, all local school administrators as masculine, regardless of actual gender of the person being considered.

2. E. R. Hilgard, *Theories of Learning* (New York: Appleton-Century-Crofts, Inc., 1956); also E. R. Gutherie, *The Psychology of Learning* (New York: Harper and Brothers Publishers, 1935); K. W. Spence, *Behavior Theory and Conditioning* (New Haven: Yale University Press, 1956).

3. W. M. Cruickshank, *The Brain-Injured Child in Home, School and Community* (Syracuse: Syracuse University Press, 1967); W. M. Cruickshank, F. A. Bentzen, F. A. Ratzeburg, and M. T. Tannhauser, *A Teaching-Method for Brain-Injured and Hyperactive Children* (Syracuse: Syracuse University Press, 1961); and W. M. Cruickshank, "The Education of the Child with Brain Injury," *Education of Exceptional Children and Youth*, eds., W. M. Cruickshank and G. O. Johnson (Englewood Cliffs: Prentice-Hall, Inc., rev. ed., 1967), Chapter 6, 238–84.

4. Fritz Redl and David Wineman, *The Aggressive Child* (New York: The Free Press of Glencoe, Inc., 1957).

5. Sheldon R. Rappaport (ed.), *Childhood Aphasia and Brain Damage: A Definition* (Narberth, Pa.: Livingston Publishing Co., 1964).

6. Ruth G. Newman and Marjorie Keith (eds.), *The School-Centered Life Space Interview* (Washington: School Research Program P.H.S. Project OM–525 Washington School of Psychiatry, 1963).

7. William M. Morse, Richard L. Cutler, and Albert H. Fink, *Public School Classes for the Emotionally Handicapped: A Research Analysis* (Washington: The Council for Exceptional Children, NEA, 1964).

8. Gerald N. Getman and E. R. Kane, *The Physiology of Readiness* (Minneapolis: Programs to Accelerate School Success, 1964).

9. N. C. Kephart, *The Slow Learner in the Classroom* (Columbus, Ohio: Charles E. Merrill Books, Inc., 1960).

10. William M. Cruickshank, "The Education of the Child with Brain Injury," *loc. cit.*

11. William M. Cruickshank, Frances A. Bentzen, Frederick H. Ratzeburg, and Miriam T. Tannhauser, *A Teaching Method for Brain-Injured and Hyperactive Children* (Syracuse: Syracuse University Press, 1961).

12. Cruickshank, "The Education of the Child with Brain Injury," *loc. cit.*

13. Cruickshank, *et al., A Teaching Method, loc. cit.*

14. William M. Cruickshank, *The Brain-Injured Child in Home, School, and Community* (Syracuse: Syracuse University Press, 1967).

CHAPTER III

Evaluation

The Syracuse University training program was geared to two major objectives. One was to make a dent in the manpower deficit of trained teachers of brain-injured children. The other was to explore the feasibility of one training strategy for the sensitization of teachers to a particular educational approach.

Relating these two objectives to the issue of evaluation, the first could probably be discarded by observing that the forty-seven teachers trained at Syracuse could hardly be viewed as a substantial force in reducing the afore-mentioned national teacher deficit. A platoon was trained and sent into the field where an army is needed.

The second objective was the more basic of the two—and the more perplexing. A body of information on the behavioral and learning characteristics of brain-injured children had been accumulated, and an educational approach had been logically formulated from an understanding of these characteristics [1, 2]. In the same sense that the educational approach had been studied to determine its effectiveness and feasibility, so the teacher-training program, as conceived, had to be viewed as an entity to be evaluated.

The question of value attached to the training program is vague. Viewed in an axiological sense, the program resisted reduction to a manageable set of questions to be answered. There were many dimensions of the training program that deserved attention, each having many parts. The process of selecting teachers to be trained, developing cooperative arrangements with school systems across the country, the determining of course work with some accommodation of the individual backgrounds of the teachers, and providing consultation to teachers and school systems based on their particular areas of need made the program extremely complex and variable.

Internal control for the purpose of securing a reasonably comparable experience was obviously not absolute. Consistency existed primarily in relation to the theoretical orientation of the senior author who directed the training program, the core professional courses, and the university structure in which the program was implemented.

Furthermore, the teachers could not be considered to be a homogeneous group, although the selection procedure attempted to include the best teachers available.

Evaluation was envisioned, therefore, as a descriptive effort to depict what happened during and after training, and three basic modes of reporting were selected: (1) group parameters along several dimensions are reported, along with comparative population parameters where possible; (2) case studies are included to point out certain issues which the authors regarded as significant; (3) a problem-solving set was utilized to try and identify as fully as possible some of the major areas deserving the attention of teacher training personnel and school administrators.

The *Minnesota Teacher Attitude Inventory* [3] was selected to obtain some indication of the special aptitudes of the teachers who were to be trained. Since they had been selected by local school system personnel who knew something of their performance in teaching, and since they had had considerable experience in the classroom which their administrators had deemed successful, they could be expected to be different from a cross-section of randomly selected teachers.

School system personnel had been asked to select teachers who had been successful in the classroom and met certain criteria (primarily personal rather than academic criteria, intuitively determined by the administrators). Would they select a unique group of teachers?

The next major block of information had to do with what happened to the trained teachers when they left the project. Again there were some obvious kinds of follow-up information that would be collected. How many teachers went back to their systems and started classes with brain-injured children? How adequately were the rooms modified? How much diagnostic service was provided? To what extent did the teacher implement the method of teaching taught in the project at Syracuse? Answers to questions like these would provide some operational kind of evaluation if the scope was conceptualized in terms of a one-to-one relation between the training project and classes established in the school systems. The unreality and limitations of this point of view became increasingly apparent. Here, it should be noted, the original base for questioning (project rationale) was modified by preliminary feedback information from initial field visits. Old questions were refined and new ones formulated, all revolving around the central question of how to best understand the feasibility of the previously described program for the university training of teachers of brain-injured children.

More often than not, university training programs for teachers are microcosmic and territorial in their focus and experience. That is, they are concentrated on classroom experience, with education being the single disciplinary concern. The education of brain-injured children, however, is a complex issue that extends beyond the conceptual and ideological framework of any one discipline. Consistent with this bias, the extent to which the training program had succeeded in incorporating an interdisciplinary framework was an issue with which the authors were greatly concerned. The availability of technical and logistical support in the systems where the teachers were expected to function after training was another, directly related to the effective implementation of interdisciplinary concepts. The territorial perspective on teachers as self-sufficient managers of self-contained classrooms had to be focused upon with a view to determining how two-way communication was established between the teachers and the other professionals within the systems. The question of the ability of school system personnel, including the teacher, to share responsibility for the entire enterprise and to somehow overcome the hurdles to communication often erected through bureaucratic substructures, was felt to be extremely important.

Since the method of education being presented required some investment of money, in modifying classrooms, for example, the question of the commitment of systems to the particular strategy of education was raised. To make the investment required in establishing adequate environments and materials along with the necessary technical support, school systems had to be committed to special education in general and to the education of brain-injured children in particular. The training program thus had to be thought of in terms of the realities of educational systems. A macrocosmic perspective, essential in conceptualizing the training program, was also basic to thinking about evaluation.

These are the kinds of questions and issues that guided the thinking about evaluation, and extended attention beyond just the university and just the teacher. The strategy of training had to be evaluated with the same macrocosmic focus. Obviously, a systems-analysis approach was required to answer the questions and to focus more sharply the questions being asked. Although such an effort was beyond the scope of the project (in fact, this point of view was not fully appreciated until rather late in the project), a compromise did seem feasible. Viewed from a system's perspective, historical, ecological, and demographic data became relevant to viewing the over-all issues in trying to appreciate the efforts of school systems to provide services to handicapped children. It seemed as much unfair as unrealistic to make superficial judgments of programs without trying to obtain as much contextual information as possible to understand the program.

While it was hoped in the beginning to make some determination of successful teachers and unsuccessful teachers after they returned to their school systems, it was found that to do this in any objective way was not possible. How does one take account of all major influences in a class? Even if criteria for success could be determined, how much of it could be attributed to the training program? What *was* possible was to describe the school systems in as much relevant detail as possible, trying to understand the teachers and their systems. The project had the distinct advantage of having an opportunity to study twenty-nine school systems in different parts of the country. They were demographically, economically, and geographically as diverse as could have been found. The philosophies of education, administrative structures, and orientation of personnel were extremely variable. This type of information, some of which relates specifically to the training program only by inference, is most useful. Some of it, the authors feel, can be shared in its own right. Its implication for teacher training, of course, is that it helps broaden the university perspective on relevance of training programs to the real world of schools in which the teachers will function. It should remind us of the limitations of a singular technical bias in training, and the information should be useful to school personnel who want to look more closely at their own systems. Finally, the perspective provided should be useful to consultants who want to maximize their own usefulness to schools and school systems.

In addition to the system perspective that has been described here, some specific information on the way in which the teacher functioned in her classes was needed. By observing the teacher in the class it was possible to determine whether or not she was using the approach to which she had been sensitized. Beyond this, the need to describe the teacher's actions objectively was evident. For this purpose the Flanders Interaction Analysis System [4] was selected. This provided some gross information on the teacher's style as an interactor in the classroom. Among other things, the Flanders provides information on certain affective characteristics of the teacher's interactions as well as on her directness. This information again seemed consistent with major aspects of the rationale.

THE FOLLOW-UP PROCESS

Each year the most recent graduates of the training program were visited twice in their own school systems. There was a complete round of visits each year for the graduates of preceding years as well (Figure 3, below).

	Years Visited			
Class	1963–64	1964–65	1965–66	1966–67
I	x x	x	x	x
II		x x	x	x
III			x x	x
IV				x

x = one visit

Figure 3.   Schema for post-training site visitations.

These field visits were viewed as attempts to understand what happened when the teachers returned to their school systems. Had classes been established for brain-injured children? Were the classrooms modified according to the rationale being used in the project?

What kind of support did the teacher have in the system? In the building where she taught? How did the system align its own resources to meet the demands of the new program? How much did other staff members in the system who logically would be involved (such as pupil personnel staff) understand the program, the admission criteria, the learning characteristics of the children, etc.? How had the program been established? Who were the most significant people related to the program? What kinds of things helped or hindered the process of establishing the class? How did the class fit into the over-all special education program? What were the future intentions of the system with respect to the class? How did the system evaluate the teachers? How did the teacher view the system? Hopefully, these questions would give some insight into the logistical, administrative, and interpersonal characteristics of systems, and some information on the discontinuity between university education and educational system realities, at least in terms of the issue of brain-injury. The question of how realistic the inclusion of such a program in an educational system is, with its particular demands for competence and commitment, is implied.

The field visits typically started with a conference with the assistant superintendent in charge of instruction or the director of special education, or both. This was followed by individual conferences with other administrative personnel such as pupil personnel services staff, the supervisor related to the class, the principal, and, of course, the teacher. At least two days, and sometimes more, were spent in such conferences trying to understand the administrative structure and the issues already described.

At least half a day was spent in the classroom observing the teacher and collecting information on the classroom itself.

An attempt has been made here to share the kinds of concerns that guided the thinking about evaluation, to indicate the nature of the information collected along with the rationale for doing so, and to describe how it was done.

THE TEACHERS

As previously mentioned, candidates were admitted to the project on the basis of meeting graduate school requirements and on the recommendations of their sending school systems. As presented to the sending systems, the qualities to have been evidenced by teacher applicants were:

Successful in small group instruction.

Skilled in one-to-one teaching situations.

Much patience.

Experimental point of view and willingness to try new methods.

Acceptant of slow progress of children.

Able to establish warm relationships between self and children.

Comfortable in a structured teaching situation.

Verbal to the point where he or she can maintain strong relationships with representatives of related disciplines.

Estimated ability to successfully handle graduate study in a research-oriented situation.

The characteristics suggested obviously required judgment based on the impressions of those selecting the teachers. The project staff members were interested in those characteristics primarily as evidenced in the classroom. Hence, the opinion of local school personnel who were supposedly familiar with the teachers' performance with children was sought. Reliance upon the judgment of these supervisory and administrative personnel seemed a reasonable strategy, within the logistical limitations of the selection process, to secure maximum probability of getting teachers with these personal and professional characteristics. The questionable validity of the assumption that local school personnel can and will select teachers along predetermined dimensions will become apparent.

DESCRIPTIVE DATA

Table I presents descriptive data on the 47 teachers. They ranged in age from 24 to 56 at the time they entered the project program, with a mean C.A. of 35 years, 6 months, and a median of 33 years, 8 months. The group was composed of 13 males and 34 females [5]. Prior teaching experience ranged from 1 to 26 years, with a mean of 7.8 years, and a median of 6.5 years. Forty-two had taught at the elementary level from 1 to 26 years, with a mean of 7.8 years. Eight had taught at the secondary level from 1 to 11 years. Of this group, five had also taught at the elementary level.

TABLE I

DESCRIPTIVE DATA ON THE GRANTEES

Class	N	Sex		Teaching Experience						Total		C.A.		MAT	
		M	F	Elementary			Secondary								
				n	Range	X̄	n	Range	X̄	Range	X̄	Range	X̄	Range	X̄
I	12	1	11	12	5–26	11.0	1	1		1–26	11.1	32–56	42.6	21–75	51.2
II	11	6	5	10	1–17	7.1	2	1–11	6.0	1–17	8.3	24–48	35.4	42–63	50.9
III	12	4	8	9	1–12	5.9	3	2–8	4.0	1–12	5.4	27–52	33.5	28–75	48.4
IV	12	2	10	11	2–12	6.6	2	2–3	2.5	2–12	6.5	24–36	30.4	27–78	45.3
Total	47	13	34	42	1–26	7.8	8	1–11	3.8	1–26	7.8	24–56	35.5	21–78	48.8

Thirty-one of the teachers held bachelor's degrees in elementary education. Six of these also held master's degrees in education. Five others with master's degrees in education, and 11 with noneducation baccalaureates had earned their undergraduate degrees in the following areas: English, history, music, music education, physical education, political science, psychology, speech correction, anthropology, biology, and industrial management (Table II).

TABLE II
DEGREES HELD BY THE TEACHERS UPON
ENTERING THE PROGRAM

Bachelor's in Education	25
Master's in Education	5
Both Bachelor's and Master's in Education	6
Other Bachelor's degrees	11
Total	47

One teacher with a bachelor's degree in music education had earned a master of social work degree. All of the teachers who were without degrees in education had taken educational coursework leading to teacher certification in their home states.

INSTRUMENTATION

During each training year, teachers were administered the *Minnesota Teacher Attitude Inventory* which purports to "measure those attitudes of a teacher which predict how well he will get along with pupils in interpersonal relationships. . . ." [6].

Due to procedural errors the MTAI scores of two teachers are not included in the following data.

Raw scores ranged from minus 21 to plus 112, with both mean and median 54.5, and a standard deviation of 27.2. Though raw scores were clustered somewhat more tightly about the mean than are those of the normative group, Figure 4 reveals that the percentile levels at which the raw scores of the teacher group fell show few differences from the norm group (whether determined by normative or teacher group parameters). In terms of the preceding information, the teacher group appears to be generally representative of a norm group of elementary teachers in systems

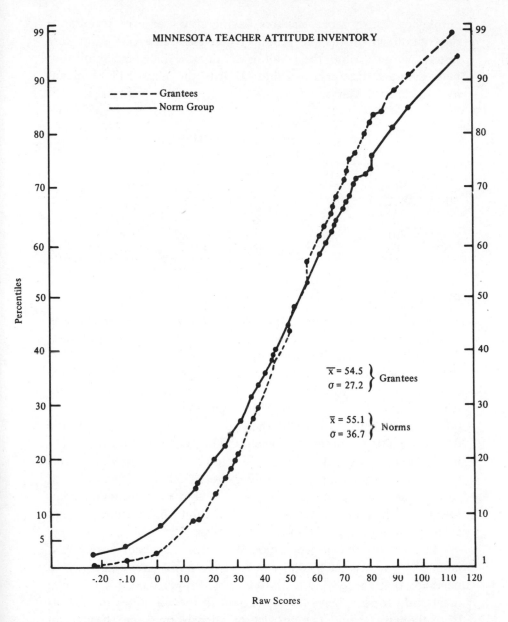

Figure 4.   MTAI percentile ranks of the teachers and a norm group.

employing 21 or more teachers having four years of training, a description which fits the group. When class MTAI means were tested, two at a time, the resulting *t* values revealed no significant between-class differences. Table III lists the class MTAI means and standard deviations.

TABLE III
CLASS MEAN SCORES ON THE *Minnesota*
Teacher Attitude Inventory

Class	Mean	Standard Deviation
I	62.58	22.96
II	43.50	35.90
III	49.33	28.99
IV	58.92	23.58

DIRECTIVENESS AND AUTHORITARIANISM

A concept of structure was basic to the rationale for teaching to which the teachers were sensitized during the training program. The teacher was viewed as the aggressive agent in classroom control, the locus of classroom direction through scheduling, and the engineer of carefully preconceived learning situations. Ambiguity was reduced to a minimum with a calculated program strategy taking precedence. Pupil alternatives were explicit, as was the decision-making source—the teacher. This was based on the teaching rationale already described. It seemed necessary, in view of this philosophic orientation, to inquire as to whether teachers able to successfully implement such a program and be reasonably comfortable with it would themselves be distinguishable along dimensions of authoritarianism and directiveness.

In terms of the project rationale, a direct teacher is one who is able to exercise such total control over pupil environments and behavior that she is able to introduce additional and different elements into these spheres as pupils gain in their abilities to deal effectively with them. The project teacher is one who has as an ultimate goal a non-directive relationship with the student, but who is capable in the interim of assuming an extremely directive role when this is needed—and this demand is an exceedingly heavy one during early stages of programming.

As used in the context of teaching brain-injured and hyperactive children, directiveness refers to the ability of the teacher to totally structure the psychological and physical environment in order to implement a program of educational intervention. The term directiveness is by no means to be confused with either dogmatism or rigidity [7]. Neither single beliefs nor systems of beliefs should have shown tendencies of closedness in the project teachers.

The *Dogmatism Scale,* a measure of general authoritarianism [8], was administered in *post hoc* fashion to 38 teachers. It was also administered for comparison purposes to full-time graduate students at master's and sixth-year specialist's levels in mental retardation, in the area of the emotionally disturbed, and in vocational rehabilitation. Table IV reports the results.

TABLE IV

DOGMATISM SCORES OF THE GRANTEES AND THREE
COMPARATIVE GROUPS

	N	$\overline{X}$	SD	t
Grantees	37	117.16	23.44	0.968
Spec. Ed.	19	123.26	22.31	
Grantees	37	117.16	23.44	2.908**
Voc. Rehab.	22	133.91	16.18	
Grantees	37	117.16	23.44	2.413*
Spec. Ed. & Voc. Rehab.	41	128.96	19.27	

* p < 0.05   ** p < 0.01

Compared with a group of full-time graduate students in special education with a mean dogmatism score of 123.26, the teacher group mean of 117.15 was not significantly lower. It was significantly lower, however, than the mean of a group of graduate students in vocational rehabilitation (p < 0.01). The latter group was composed mainly of individuals from disciplines other than education, whereas the special education group was made up of trained and experienced teachers. A difference in test administration procedures is noted here: The special education and vocational rehabilitation groups responded under conditions of anonymity, while the project teachers were not allowed to do so.

A general absence of between-group differences thus became apparent when comparisons were made of the teacher group and other groups of experienced teachers who had responded either to the MTAI or the Dogmatism Scale. In the case of the MTAI the within-group differences of both the teachers and the norm group ran courses which were almost parallel (see Figure 4).

SYSTEM SELECTION PROCEDURES

As indicated by Table V, 20 teachers were sent by systems which had solicited applications from their personnel. Seventeen other teachers were pre-selected. The remaining 10 teachers initiated their own applications, and their systems subsequently entered into the necessary commitments with the training project.

A total figure for school systems was not entered in Table V,

TABLE V
HOW THE TEACHERS WERE SELECTED
BY THE SENDING SYSTEMS

Selection Mode	No. of Systems	N
Solicitation of applicants	8	20
Pre-selection	15	17
Teacher-initiated	8	10
Total	a	47

a Some systems used more than one selection mode.

as some systems eventually used more than one selection mode. The sending agencies were actually 28 public school systems and one private school located in 15 states.

Table VI reflects the mean MTAI scores of the teachers when grouped according to system selection modes.

The mean MTAI score of the teachers who were selected from groups of solicited applicants was 43.42. The mean MTAI score of the teachers who were pre-selected by their systems was 60.13.

TABLE VI
MTAI Scores of Teachers Grouped by
System Selection Modes

Selection Mode	X̄ MTAI	S.D.	t
Solicitation	43.42	25.31	2.94**
Self-initiated	71.22	14.83	
Pre-selection	60.13	23.72	

** p < 0.01

For the teachers who initiated their own applications, the mean MTAI score was 71.22. In addition to the trend indicated by the direction in which these means increased, the difference between the solicited group and the self-initiated group was significant (p < 0.01).

There were no significant differences between mean scores of these groups on the Dogmatism Scale. The dogmatism data are incomplete, however, as results were obtained from only 38 teachers.

THE SENDING SYSTEMS

The sending systems spanned wide ranges in terms of populations, financial resources, socio-economic composition, politico-educational orientation, and commitment to services for exceptional children. These variables were directly reflected in the extent to which systems were able to—or decided to—establish and support project-type classes upon the return of their teachers.

The small school districts served cities ranging in populations from 20,000 to approximately 45,000.

The medium-sized city school districts ranged in populations from 85,000 to approximately 300,000. All had experienced changes in population characteristics in the preceding few years which led to problems directly affecting the public schools.

The large city school districts, with populations ranging from 700,000 to in excess of three million, had all experienced problems stemming from social changes within the cities. As with the bulk of communities connected with the Syracuse training project, internal funding issues were of paramount importance, characterized by increasing expenses and decreasing ability to meet them.

One board of cooperative services provided special education programs and facilities to a group of small cities, townships and villages. A second board owned, staffed, and operated special education facilities for over 90 separate municipalities suburban to a large midwestern city. A third cooperative board coordinated and supervised special education programs operated by an association of school districts in one of the nation's largest centers of population.

Three county school districts were suburban in character, containing populations from about 100,000 to 200,000. All were "bedroom" type communities, although two extended into rural areas. Another county district was entirely rural in character, serving a small city and its surrounding hamlets.

The single private sending agency was an order of Roman Catholic teaching nuns desirous of establishing an educational program for brain-injured children.

ORGANIZATIONAL STRUCTURE

With a single exception, all of the school systems contained within their organizational structures a department dealing specifically with special education. A vast range in scope, responsibility, and authority existed among these subdivisions. Some were entitled, "Department of Special Education." Others, rather than having titles, were identified through the titles of their chief officers (e.g., Director, or Supervisor of Special Education).

In addition to the chief special education official, some systems had intermediary administrative/supervisory personnel between the chief official and the classroom teachers and specialists. The systems varied in this respect from one with an essentially informal working arrangement between a psychometrist and the superintendent of schools, to several with heavily structured bureaus of special education headed by assistant superintendents and containing many high, intermediate and low echelon administrative, supervisory, and coordinating positions.

Most of the systems operated educational services for the mentally retarded, the hard-of-hearing, and the visually handicapped.

In addition, some had programs for orthopedic or multiply handicapped children. A few had educational programs for brain-injured children at the time they sent their teachers to the Syracuse University training project.

PUPIL SERVICES

System substructures addressed to pupil services varied from meticulously articulated bureaus headed and staffed by directors, psychologists, social workers, and guidance personnel, to those employing a single psychometrist. Most of the systems had at least one full-time psychologist on their staffs, and many had more. Almost none had guidance services specifically directed to elementary school pupils. Approximately one-half had social work services relating in some degree to their special education programs.

PROGRAMS

The systems especially differed in the services they offered to children marked by negatively atypical learning or behavioral characteristics. At the time the teachers returned to their schools, six systems already had programs for brain-injured children. Eight systems (including two of the six) had programs for emotionally disturbed children. The remaining systems had never before attempted to serve these groups with public school programs.

Of the twenty-nine systems, sixteen had published mimeographed descriptions of their programs, including pupil selection criteria. Eight of the thirteen systems which had not done this were ones which had sent their teachers to the final training class. During their on-site visitations (perforce during the fall semester of the project's final year) most explained that they were in the process of doing so.

The descriptive statements of twenty-three systems were couched in terms of brain injury, perceptual handicaps, learning disabilities, or other commonly used appellations suggestive of neurological dysfunction. Five systems addressed their program descriptions to behaviorally deviant children, with no references whatsoever to psychopathology as a criterion base.

Post-Training Disposition of the Teachers

During the five-year existence of the training project the four training classes were followed for four years, three years, two years, and one year, respectively, after returning to their school systems.

As shown in Figure 5, there were only two intervening years between the initial and final follow-up years of Class I, and one for Class II. An examination of Figure 6, which presents the year-by-year post-training disposition of the teachers will show that in only a single case (II–9) did a position held by one of the teachers in an intervening year differ from the one held in either the initial or final years.

Year	1962–63	1963–64	1964–65	1965–66	1966–67
Class					
I		x	x	x	x
II			x	x	x
III				x	x
IV					x

Figure 5.   Initial, intervening, and final follow-up years of the project.

A few returning teachers were absorbed directly into existing programs for brain-injured children; others were assigned to newly established classes for emotionally disturbed children; several returned as administrators; a small number returned to conventional pre-training teaching assignments; the largest number returned to established programs for brain-injured children where none had before existed.

Table VII depicts the positions the teachers occupied during their initial post-training years and during the final year of the project. "Project Context" is defined as any position which relates professionally to the education of brain-injured and hyperactive children. Though local pupil selection criteria varied to some extent, the teachers included under this heading were able, with varying degrees of success, to establish and employ project-type models in their work.

"Non-Project Context" subsumes all occupational roles other than those connected with brain-injured and hyperactive children, including teachers of classes of emotionally disturbed children.

		1962–63	1963–64	1964–65	1965–66	1966–67
Class I	1	Teacher	Teacher	Teacher	Teacher
	2	Teacher[a]	Teacher	Teacher	Teacher
	3	Teacher	Teacher	Teacher	Teacher
	4	Consultant	Consultant	Consultant	Consultant
	5	Teacher	Graduate[a] Student	Teacher[a]	Teacher[a]
	6	Teacher	Teacher	Teacher	Teacher
	7	Teacher	Teacher	Teacher	Teacher
	8	Teacher	Teacher	Teacher	Teacher
	9	Graduate Student[a]	Teacher	Teacher	Supervisor
	10	Teacher	Teacher	Teacher	Teacher
	11	Speech Therapist[a]	Speech Therapist[a]	Speech Therapist[a]	Teacher[a]
	12	Teacher	Teacher	Teacher	Teacher
Class II	1		Teacher	Teacher	Teacher[a]
	2		Teacher	Teacher	Dean-Women[a]
	3		Teacher[a]	Teacher[a]	Teacher[a]
	4		Teacher	Teacher	Teacher
	5		Teacher	Supervisor	Director
	6		Teacher	Teacher	Teacher
	7		Teacher[a]	Teacher[a]	Teacher
	8		Teacher	Teacher	Teacher
	9		Consultant[a]	Teacher[a]	Research
	10		Teacher[a]	Teacher[a]	Teacher[a]
	11		Non-Educator[a]	Non-Educator[a]	Non-Educator[a]
Class III	1			Teacher	Teacher
	2			Teacher[a]	Diagnostician
	3			Teacher	Teacher
	4			Teacher[a]	Teacher[a]
	5			Teacher	Teacher
	6			Supervisor	Supervisor
	7			Teacher	Graduate Student[a]
	8			Teacher[a]	Teacher
	9			Teacher	Teacher
	10			Teacher[a]	Teacher[a]
	11			Teacher	Reading Supervisor[a]
	12			Teacher	Teacher
Class IV	1				Teacher
	2				Teacher
	3				Teacher
	4				Teacher
	5				Teacher
	6				Teacher
	7				Teacher
	8				Teacher
	9				Teacher
	10				Teacher
	11				Teacher
	12				Teacher

[a] Non-Project Context.

Figure 6. Post-training positions of the teachers.

TABLE VII
INITIAL AND FINAL POST-TRAINING YEAR DISPOSITION
OF THE TEACHERS

| | | Project Context | | Non-Project Context | | |
| | | | | (3) As Teacher of Emotionally | (4) In Other | |
Year	Class	(1) As Teacher	(2) In Other Capacity	Disturbed	Capacity	Total
Initial						
1963–64	I	8	1	1	2	12
1964–65	II	6	0	3	2	11
1965–66	III	7	1	3	1	12
1966–67	IV	12	0	0	0	12
Sub-Total		33	2	7	5	
Total		35		12		47
Per cent		75		25		100
Final						
	I	8	2	2	0	12
	II	4	2	0	5	11
1966–67						
	III	6	2	1	3	12
	IV	12	0	0	0	12
Sub-Total		30	6	3	8	
Total		36		11		47
Per cent		77		23		100

Thirty-three of the teachers were employed as teachers of brain-injured children in the initial post-training years. Two others returned as administrators in programs dealing with brain-injured children. Thus, the number of teachers dealing with brain-injured children during the initial post-training years was 35, or 75 per cent of the total group. Seven other returning teachers were employed as teachers of emotionally disturbed children (including some who were mentally retarded). One taught orthopedically handicapped children, three were in positions only tangentially related to any phase of special education (e.g., teaching a "slow" seventh grade English class), and one left the field of education completely. These twelve teachers constituted 25 per cent of the group.

These percentages remained the same during the final post-training year, although the roles of some teachers had changed in the interim. By the final year, three of the teachers of emotionally disturbed children had become teachers of brain-injured children, as had the teacher of orthopedically handicapped children. Thus, during the four-year post-training follow-up period, 37 of the teachers served at least one year in the classroom with brain-injured children, and four other teachers moved into administrative positions. While the original two administrators were still with their sending systems, the new administrators had received appointments in other systems.

Only one of three teachers in the Initial section of Column 3 is reflected in the Final section of that column. Four had moved into project-contexted positions (Columns 1 and 2) and two had reverted to pre-training teaching assignments (Column 4). Of the other two teachers in the Final section of Column 3, one had initially been a teacher of brain-injured children (Column 1) and one had initially been employed in another capacity (Column 4).

THE MAJOR NEEDS OF THE TEACHERS

It was the general consensus of the teachers that, from a technical standpoint, they had returned well-prepared to organize and teach their classes. Some had been forced to revise the content of their instructional materials when older children were placed in their classes, and all were forced to devise and manufacture additional materials to meet daily needs, but the specifics of pupil selection and the control and sequencing of stimuli remained constant.

The most immediately pressing need reported by the teachers was assistance in the preparation of the staggering amounts of instructional materials which were needed daily. Many of the teachers had the part- or full-time services of an assistant, and had trained these assistants in the reproduction of materials, but each item or series of items had to be planned by the teachers themselves.

Many instructional items for pupils with attention spans of one or two minutes took fifteen or twenty minutes to prepare. The prodigious rates at which these individualized materials were used can readily be imagined. A few items could be reproduced routinely, but the most important ones—especially as programs advanced—required the full attention of the teachers. Many teachers found themselves spending every weekday evening and one full day each weekend in designing and manufacturing instructional materials. These pressures slackened only slightly in successive teaching years. Although these logistical needs had been addressed *in kind* in the training program, the *degree* to which they were to become major post-training variables was not anticipated.

The post-training demands which were not specifically provided for in the training program were largely extramural in nature, and revolved around the personality characteristics and interpersonal skills needed by the teachers in establishing effective relationships with other professionals and with local sources of system power and influence.

Historically, educational provisions for exceptional children have come into existence largely because of pressures mounted by parent groups. The collective voices of taxpayers and voters succeeded in sensitizing local educators to the presence of groups of children who were not being adequately provided for in the public schools. Decisions to inaugurate new programs were translated into demands that universities and colleges of education provide teachers with the appropriate training. In response to these demands the few existing teacher-training programs were expanded and many new ones were begun with the help of public funding.

The same dynamics pertain to the establishment of educational programs for brain-injured children. At this writing, the parent groups have just passed through their initial stages of organization, and they are beginning to make their influence felt. Increasingly, educators at all levels will begin concentrating on building programs for brain-injured children, and training the teachers to staff these programs.

The fact that this had not yet happened when the teachers returned to their systems over the four-year period 1963 to 1966 had far-reaching implications for the situations they faced upon returning.

Only a few returned to systems which were already attempting to provide programs for brain-injured children. Considerable confusion and many differing points of view were present in these systems. The returning teachers brought with them philosophical orientations that were often in conflict with established thinking.

Most of the teachers returned as local pioneers in their fields of newly-gained expertise. With some administrative help many of the teachers aggressively pursued the establishment of conditions which would help the systems to *find* their brain-injured children, and allow the teachers to teach them.

What were the results of these efforts?

System Support

Of the forty teachers who functioned as teachers after returning (see Initial totals of Columns 1 and 3 of Table VII), 32 per cent were eventually given the services of full-time classroom assistants; 41 per cent had part-time assistants, and 22 per cent had no aide services whatsoever.

(The teachers of emotionally disturbed classes are included in this accounting because their systems provided them with many of the plant and personnel resources advocated by the training project. The inability of some system administrators to conceptualize educational programs for behaviorally deviant children of *any* type will be described and discussed later.)

Eighty-one per cent of these teachers taught in classrooms which for the most part had been appropriately modified in terms of project specifications (most general omission: floor carpeting), 12 per cent were in partially modified rooms, and 3 teachers (7 per cent) were in conventional classrooms with no modifications at all.

Seventy-three per cent of the classrooms were in locations which were generally free of outside visual or auditory distractions, 25 per cent were subjected to minor distractions at various times during each day, and one classroom was in a completely inappropriate location, constantly bombarded by outside noises.

The priorities which the systems had allocated to the classroom space of these programs were another indication of the extent to which they were committed to programming for brain-injured children. Sixty-one per cent of the teachers were in systems which had assigned them space priorities on a par with all other local programs. The remaining 39 per cent were in systems where space priorities were of the lowest, and where the classrooms were frequently moved in the face of other space demands.

In addition to seeking the obviously necessary logistical support, the teachers found themselves making overwhelming energy investments in seeking modifications in the roles of other professionals connected with their programs. They were almost invariably confronted by issues of disciplinary territoriality, that is, conventional or traditional assignment of function. They had to take upon themselves the task of convincing administrators and diagnosticians of the need for specific information on their incoming pupils, and for the need of teacher-involvement in the pupil selection process. Some of the teachers were highly successful in these attempts, some were moderately successful, and some were unsuccessful.

During a post-training seminar attended by about two-thirds of the teachers, the teachers' need for ability to explain and effectively promote the program locally, and the need for effective channels of communication was universally manifested.

Thirty-seven per cent of the teachers functioned at peer levels with diagnostic, evaluation, and placement staffs. An additional 22 per cent were allowed to attend staffing conferences to either contribute or glean whatever information was available. Forty-one per cent were permitted no involvement whatsoever in the identification or selection of their pupils.

PSYCHOLOGICAL SERVICES

There was a wide range of differences in the psychological services offered by the systems. Quantitatively they ranged from a system served by a part-time psychometrist, to one with a staff of full-time clinicians headed by a chief psychologist.

Fifteen systems employed two or more full-time psychologists. Nine each had a single psychologist. Three systems were serviced only by psychometrists. Two employed no psychological staff whatsoever but purchased certain services from nearby universities.

Those systems which had access to local non-system clinics or diagnostic facilities made what use of them they were able (usually by referring parents to them as private clients), but this type of relationship was so sporadic, both within and between systems, that no attempt will be made here to report on it.

Without exception, the systems' psychological personnel had staggeringly heavy case loads. The bulk of their time was spent in routine testing and re-testing required by their state departments of education. All too frequently these personnel had to almost literally "make time" to work in depth with pupils in need of diagnostic services. Regardless of case loads, however, all of the pupils placed in the teachers' classes had received some type of assessment. The value to the teacher of the reports which stemmed from these assessments varied. The following are examples of the types of reports received.

Report A

A Rorschach was administered to ———. His contact with a reality situation appeared borderline. ——— appeared to be an arbitrary youngster with fairly weak drive. His personality appears to be constricted, conflicted and anxious. He seems to be an immature youngster who had difficulty in interpersonal relationships.

A parent conference should be held and these results discussed with them. ——— needs some professional assistance with his emotional problems.

Report B

Has a low dull normal ability; achievement is at or slightly above present mental age. Seems to be very poor social and emotional development. [sic] All Bender drawings were reproduced fairly well and accurately in relation to his Binet and Wechsler scores and were near the level expected in relation to his chronological age. The irregularities and findings were significant psychologically; there were signs that he is egocentric, aggressive, is inclined to act out his impulses for the immediate gratifications of his needs.

Report C

An individual test of intelligence showed a fluctuating test pattern, typical of a child with visuo-perceptual deficits. ———'s scores ranged from 5 in Picture Completion, 6 in Object Assembly and 6 in Arithmetic to scores of 14 in Similarities, 12 in Comprehension and 11 in Information. He was tense, fidgity and jittery, with a slight hand tremor clearly noted in wavy lines on the Coding task. He tended to give up easily and act on impulse; he had poor control of blocks, puzzle pieces, etc. He had poor perception of sequential patterns and relationships. He had difficulty with visual concentration, unable to filter out distracting stimuli. His auditory memory was good, when he was attending. ———— had achieved cerebral dominance, preferring his right side consistently. His gross motor control is good. ————'s handwriting, drawings and other written work reflects a generalized disorganization of responses, particularly those which are dependent upon the integration of visual-perceptual processes.

Reports A and B were typical of the kinds of information that many teachers were given to use as bases for program planning. Report A tells the teacher very little about the pupil that the referring teacher did not already know. The same is true of Report B, unless the fact that "The irregularities and findings were significant psychologically . . . ," may have been helpful.

Report C begins to describe psychopathological characteristics and indicates that the pupil under study is probably a bona fide candidate for placement, but it lacks the detailed reporting a receiving teacher would need to begin planning for the child. (Report C did in fact serve as the basis for an information exchange between psychologist and the teacher during which many more specifics were brought to light.)

The general caliber of much of the reporting, plus the extent to which many psychologists were overcommitted, led to the question of how certain systems had been able to properly identify and place brain-injured children in their classes.

The three systems to be reported upon next typify groups of other systems in that each contained various personnel who displayed initiative in overcoming placement-staffing deficiencies. The reports will focus on an administrator, a teacher, and two psychologists.

A DYNAMIC ADMINISTRATOR

A city with a public school population of approximately 70,000 employed four psychologists. The activities of the psychologists were largely limited to the standardized administration of individual intelligence tests. The factor mainly responsible for the proper identification and placement of pupils in that system's classes for brain-injured children appeared to be the close communication which the local director of special education established between himself and the teacher well before the opening of any new classes. In the spring of the teacher's training year the director began communicating with her in preparation for working together during the ensuing summer. That summer the teacher was able to examine historical, educational, and diagnostic information which had been accumulated on pupils under consideration for placement in her class. By the time the class opened in the fall the teacher—working with the director, and through him with the psychologists—had been able to select from a pool of candidates those children who appeared to have the greatest potential for profiting from the program to be inaugurated in the classroom.

A DYNAMIC TEACHER

A suburban school district serving 30,000 pupils employed two psychologists. The returning teacher had long and successful experience in almost every aspect of public school teaching. Because of long years of mutually satisfying professional relationships between the teacher and the administration, policy was established enabling the teacher to become involved in the pupil selection process on an equal footing with the system's diagnosticians. The teacher was given the opportunity to observe candidates in their present classrooms and to report her findings to the placement committee, which in turn incorporated them into their final staffing conferences.

TWO PRAGMATIC PSYCHOLOGISTS

In a large city, two psychologists were responsible for the diagnosis and placement of brain-injured children from a school population in excess of 500,000. Although the system employed other psychologists, these were assigned to groups of schools by geographic areas, and were unavailable for any diagnostic services beyond the broad-screening type of early identification stemming from teacher referrals.

The two psychologists had extensive backgrounds of clinical training and experience, although they were overworked and over-extended. With literally hundreds of potential brain-injured class candidates in their files, and recognizing both the limited number of class vacancies occurring each year and the great lapse in time which typically took place between selection and actual placement, these individuals realistically, if perforce somewhat cynically, re-frained from becoming deeply involved with individual pupils until and unless an actual placement vacancy appeared imminent. The result was that while an enormously large school system was serving only a pitifully small number of brain-injured children, those in the program had been appropriately identified.

Other systems benefited from the presence of personnel of similar caliber who were able to help the systems to circumvent their own built-in staffing deficiencies. Typical of these personnel were the following types:

1. A sophisticated special education administrator, willing and able to establish and maintain effective communication be-tween psychologists and teachers.

2. A very strong teacher, able to establish local precedents in relating to other disciplines.

3. Competent psychologists, able to deal effectively with the logistical facts of life.

The foregoing is not meant to suggest that these were the only capable people present in the systems, but it is meant to indicate—unequivocally—the needs many systems have both for adequate psychological services and for personnel with the initiative to com-pensate for staffing deficiencies. A further discussion of system dynamics will be found in the final chapter of this report.

The programs for brain-injured children begun by project teachers in a small number of systems developed strong roots through the deep involvement of local personnel. Almost invariably found in these systems were one or more administrators with enough relevant experience and sophistication to have developed *certain awareness* of local needs. In addition, most of these indi-viduals were capable evaluators. It is not meant here that they were all intimately familiar with the specifics of educating brain-injured children, but they were extremely competent generalists, able to give guidance and general supervision to their teachers. The programs presented no mystique to these administrators; only a rationale-anchored education strategy to watch. They were careful to lay detailed groundwork for the new programs. Steps were taken to insure that other personnel associated with the programs were aware of their own roles and of what was to be requested of them. Channels of communication were examined and, where necessary, were restructured or opened. Above all, they planned for optimal teacher involvement in every aspect of the programs, from intake to reintegration.

This last was accomplished by some of the administrators only at great effort. For the first time in many of the systems medical, paramedical, and pupil service personnel found themselves asked to include classroom teachers in their collective deliberations—not only as observers, but as participants with voting privileges! Again, territorial issues emerged in different forms and had to be dealt with openly. It is to the credit of these administrators and most of the professionals with whom they worked that the welfare of children was recognized as having precedence over all other differences.

MOTOR TRAINING PROGRAM

Figures 7 through 13 are presented at this point as an aid in the visualization of a portion of the teachers' programs which may be less familiar to the reader than some of their more recognizably academic segments. The literature relating motor training to academic achievement is admittedly inconclusive, although there is much to suggest that there may be a positive correlation between the two. There is not enough in the literature, however, to support the more extreme claims which are sometimes made for programs which rely heavily on motor activity. Furthermore, in relation to the present teacher-preparation program, the elements of motor training were not included in the program of Class I, and were present in only a very limited manner for the students of Class II. The developing interest in the problem of motor training by professional persons concerned with the education of hyperactive and brain-injured children made itself sufficiently known to warrant its discussion in the program of Class II, but it did not receive a major emphasis in the training program until the beginning of the year with Class III. Students in Classes III and IV not only received theoretical background for the motor training program, but also engaged in extensive supervised motor training experiences with the demonstration class children. The fact that this phase of the over-all program was not universally experienced by all four training classes prevented its inclusion as an aspect of the total evaluation effort.

The 24 teachers in Classes III and IV were able to implement programs of motor training with various degrees of effectiveness. From extremely well conceived entities, parts of which are depicted in Figures 7 through 13, these ranged down to some in which motor training was only superficially present. In a few classrooms, this aspect of child development was not programmed at all. The presence of this part of the total program related directly to the availability of space, funds, auxiliary personnel, and administrative understanding and support.

Environmental Planning

Figures 14 through 28 have been included in this report to illustrate some of the modifications which school systems made in order to house the special education programs. Modifications were made in nearly every classroom to which teachers returned. In selecting the illustrations presented in this section, no attempt has been made to select examples of either poor or good learning situations. No criticism is intended in the comments which accompany them. The photographs were selected to depict the varying ways in which the systems interpreted project recommendations, and the extent to which they were able to follow them. Each school system approached this problem in terms of its own financial resources and general understanding of the theory and methodology recommended.

The photographs represent one major problem which faced many teachers and principals as they tried to align the educational environment with educational theory. While the teacher-principal requests for room modifications were usually appropriate, the interpretation of these requests by plant administrators and buildings and grounds staff members often resulted in violations of the very guidelines which had been followed in planning the modifications. The use of high-gloss paint or varnish, the use of chrome hardware, the choice of furniture, the retention of venetian blinds, and

Figure 7. Gross motor training with a small group of children. Teacher serving as a guide for child during early phases of training program. Note visual target placed on post.

other similar types of non-educational decisions sometimes resulted in an educational environment far different from that recommended or desired by the teachers. The necessity for incorporating construction personnel into the educational planning, and of insuring that they thoroughly understand exactly what is desired, became obvious to project personnel as classroom visits were made.

Figure 8. Balance board activity. While the teacher observes, two children assist one another in maintaining balance. The beginning of small group activity is employed here as a normal part of the specialized training program.

TYPICAL POST-TRAINING EXPERIENCES

RETURNING TO AN ESTABLISHED PROGRAM

Three systems were comparable in several respects. They all served very large populations. They all had programs in operation for brain-injured children before their teachers entered the Syracuse training project. They all had full ranges of pupil personnel services. All of the principals with whom the teachers worked during their first post-training year had attended the administrators' seminar.

Figure 9. Gross motor training utilizing walking board and balance rod. Visual target appears on post. Child appears cautious and uncertain, and needs balance rod at this stage of development.

While pupil intake procedures differed somehwat, those who were actually placed in the special classes largely satisfied project selection criteria.

One system was a city school district, one was a county school district, and one was a cluster of city school districts served by a board of cooperative services. In spite of these differences, all of the systems contained similar pupil personnel service processes. In each, school psychologists and visiting teachers (social workers) made initial contacts with pupils based upon referrals from teachers and principals. They then performed initial work-up services, sub-

Figure 10.   Gross motor training involving two levels of walking rails with no balance assistance.

sequently turning their information over to an evaluation-placement body. Though these bodies ranged in size from a single person to a large committee, and though only one system involved its teacher in the pupil placement process, the bulk of pupils in the project teachers' classes met project criteria.

The school principals in these systems operated under conditions of considerable autonomy, and were allowed much latitude in implementing educational policies within their schools. The limits of this latitude were in large part determined by their initiative and willingness to assume responsibility and to test their systems' limits

Figure 11. Teacher helping a child to prepare herself for gross motor activity integrating visual and motor functions.

in obtaining whatever they thought was needed for the educational programs under their jurisdictions.

The school principals who were involved with project teachers spanned the full range—including both extremes—of a continuum focused on their own safety levels. A few perceived themselves as administrators of essentially static facilities which had long had their operating groundrules established; change or innovation was unwelcome, if not feared. These principals invariably felt threatened by the additional stresses caused by the presence of special classes in their buildings. They were hesitant about making new, addi-

Figure 12. Gross motor training linking motor activity, judgment of spatial relationships, and recognition of numerals. Here teacher assists child in maintaining balance until he can develop his own coordinated movements.

tional, or unusual requests for supplies, equipment, or services. Special transportation problems, nonexistent with regular class pupils, were a particular threat. In this context one principal verbalized vociferously about the "unfairness of being caught in the middle, between parents and the administration." These principals usually had only minimal contacts with their special classes or the teachers in them.

Other principals appeared to have assimilated their special classes with few signs of stress. Though faced with the same sets

Figure 13. Child, now capable of accurate self-direction, engaged in visual motor activity utilizing gross motor functions.

of problems as the others (many of whom were in the same systems), these individuals had rapidly made heavy investments in familiarizing themselves with the new program, its goals, design, and pupils. Logistical problems were addressed with a routine matter-of-factness which implied that while they were important issues, they were only incidental to the real business of education. Though these kinds of problems were not always solved to the complete satisfaction of the project teachers involved, the teachers who worked with these principals appeared able to take such disappointments in stride.

Figure 14. Many elements of this classroom setting follow the recommended design, but here the educators were unable to maintain control over the buildings and grounds department which did the construction. Hence the finished product was a highly stimulating cubicle which resulted from exposed wood grain, high-gloss varnish, and moldings of different color from the cubicle wall. Wall-to-wall carpeting is used to assimilate stimuli created within the room. Lighting is not completely satisfactory in that shadows will be created over the child's work when he bends forward at his desk.

Regardless of the supportive roles played by principals, those in one of the three systems were unable to effect any influence on the rate at which pupils were brought into newly established programs. The reasons for staggered enrollment had been made clear to all concerned, but while upper-echelon administrators professed agreement in principle, they reported themselves unable to resist pressures from parents and other potent sources of influence in their community, with the result that all classes were at full strength before the end of the first month of school.

One of the three systems employed a curriculum consultant for the program which dealt with brain-injured children. This individual was responsible for instructional programming, for advising teachers in the areas of classroom management and the preparation

Figure 15. Ceiling detail of cubicles shown in Figure 14. With the exception of the exposed wood grain, this construction has many positive aspects.

of instructional materials, for in-service training, and for the resolution of other problems specific to the program.

Because of the large size of the system, a nominal rate of teacher turnover and the addition of new classes kept the curriculum coordinator extremely busy in providing guidance, training, and supervision to new or inexperienced teachers assigned to the program. On top of these demands, the coordinator was expected to incorporate into the program a group of teachers possessing an orientation which, while in general agreement with the existing one, had some very evident differences.

Relations between the project teachers and the coordinator eventually became determined in part by the tenacity and interpersonal skills with which the project teachers pursued their requests for system support. Some of the project teachers proved to be adamant in their support demands, while others reflected varying degrees of passivity.

The aggressive teachers, in spite of support deficiencies, succeeded to a considerable extent in putting project-type programs

Figure 16. Detail of room shown in Figure 14. Enclosed cupboards follow program recommendations, but once again buildings and grounds department implementation has violated educational concepts. Wood grain, exposed hinges, lower wood panels with vertical lines all add to pupils' environmental distractions. The open cupboard at lower left is for illustrative purposes only, to indicate the necessity of closed cupboards and shelves for the reduction of their stimulus values.

into operation. Classroom space was organized in keeping with project rationale as closely as possible. Walls were free of stimulating materials and windows were covered either by shades or with heavy paper. Instruction was individualized. Learning tasks and seat work activities were tailored specifically to the current needs of each pupil. Teacher assistants, when available, were used for the preparation of instructional materials. High degrees of pupil alternative-choice control were initially maintained by these teachers. Educational diagnoses had been performed by these teachers on almost every pupil. Motor training programs were in effect, despite a general absence of formal equipment. Positive affective relationships existed between these teachers and their pupils. Pupils were seldom at a loss for "things to do" when immediate assignments were completed and the teachers were busy elsewhere. Classrooms appeared generally tension-free, with pupils able to proceed independently to

Figure 17. Modifiable cubicles intended to permit adjustment of room to varying needs of the children and the educational program. This situation has many advantages and is in keeping with some of the program recommendations. It is more satisfactory for children who are being considered for return to the regular grades than it is for children newly placed in the clinical teaching situation.

additional work assignments. The following case studies are representative of teachers who returned to the three systems which were already operating programs for brain-injured children. Some of the information in the studies will be supported by classroom interaction data to be presented in a later section of this chapter.

T–32's classroom was a pleasant, unusually quiet yet active place. There were six children in the class, with another one absent. Each child was busy at work, three in cubicles and three at a table.

The psychological as well as the physical environment seemed comfortable (see interaction analysis).

T–32 had been aggressive in controlling pupil intake, stating (during on-site visit) that if the board of education knew she had only 7 children in her class, several more would soon be coming; so she does not tell them. In this way she is able to work with a manageable group of children. She had adequate materials which she had obtained largely through her own initiative. T–32 described a very positive relationship

Fgure 18. Hinge detail for cubicles shown in Figure 17. Note large space between back and side walls. In this situation buildings and grounds department insisted on installation of very expensive chrome-plated hinges which ultimately had to be painted over to reduce pupil distraction. This situation is illustrative of the detailed communication involvement that may exist between educators and technicians. All too frequently misguided goodwill on the part of technicians can add to the childrens' problems.

between herself and the school principal. She pictured the principal as very supportive of the class and actively involved in trying to understand the work going on in it. The observer got the same impression upon talking with the principal. He seemed knowledgeable regarding the classroom activities (although not having attended the SU seminar), very positive in his attitudes toward T–32 and her work, and matter-of-fact regarding discipline problems that arise and eventually involve him as principal.

This is in sharp contrast to the school principal in whose building T–32's class was located the previous year. This individual (who had attended the seminar) had felt extremely threatened by the presence of T–32's class and had given it minimal support.

An interesting aspect here is the general acceptance of the learning impairments program in this school.

Very obviously the administrators of the school system "knew" the size of this teacher's class. The adjacent class, with which this

Figure 19.   Detail showing floor catch of the cubicles illustrated in Figure 17.

teacher had such a good relationship, was of similar size. Most of the other learning impairment classes in the system contained between 10 and 15 pupils. The professional aggressiveness displayed by these two teachers, coupled with the support given by the building principal seemed to be the essential elements in this program's development. These teachers were largely left alone by the program coordinator, who had many other demands upon his services and time. The two teachers were generally better supplied than any of the other project teachers in that system. Like most teachers, they had spent personal funds for some materials, but more important, they and their principal had requested, begged, cajoled and threatened until they were able to obtain a minimum of supplies and materials from the system itself.

In sharp contrast to these individuals were two others in the same system whose classrooms, after several years of operation, showed little sign of project influence.

T–10's principal seemed to know little about exactly what T–10 was doing, but appeared to be politely accepting of the program. The classroom had not been modified in any way. There were 14 children in the class. T–10's manner was excessively polite with the children, but the

Figure 20. Cubicles constructed with most details of project recommendations being followed. The height of these cubicles and the general feeling of massiveness may be criticized as inappropriate in view of the fact that many hyperactive and brain-injured children find it difficult to deal with large amounts of space. The walls of these cubicles are covered with a very fine-grained wallpaper, a factor which for some children might cause an attention problem. With these exceptions these cubicles are very satisfactory. Note that they are large enough to permit a teacher to sit at the side of a child for individual instruction, or at other times to permit two children to utilize the same cubicle. This permits the teacher to observe the children under condition of greater stimulation as a first step toward return to regular class placement.

observer sensed an uncomfortable hostility in her relationships with them. A delayed response from a child when given a direction seemed to raise the tension level considerably. It was difficult to find any specific examples of the approach to teaching advocated by the training project. Both visual and auditory backgrounds in the classrooms were gross.

T–10 reported little support from the local board of education. Her class had just this year moved from another building because of space considerations. Her new principal had not attended the administrators' seminar. The teacher stated that although three of the pupils would probably be ready for regular class re-integration by the following fall, the waiting list was such that the vacancies would be "quickly filled."

Figure 21. Detail showing ceiling and lighting arrangements. The presence of external light fixtures, multiple angles, pipes, and wooden frames all add to the visual distractions with which pupils must cope. The recommended educational program would require much further thought regarding these details.

The primary education intervention here appeared to be reduced class size (14 rather than 35). Whereas T–10 was not happy about the size of her class, she had not taken any noticeable action to change the situation. Lack of materials seemed to be a major concern, but nothing had been done by the teacher to remedy the matter.

T–10's principal confessed total ignorance of the program (in the spring of the school year), and only hoped that the class could become a little better ordered. His main concerns regarding the class were for transportation problems, scheduling, and pupil discipline.

There are 11 children in T–45's classroom. A full-time assistant is present in the room. The room has been appropriately modified. T–45's class is new in the building, having been moved this year from another

Figure 22. A modified classroom. Figures 22 through 28 illustrate a non-classroom which has been converted and modified into a classroom for brain-injured and hyperactive children. The above view is from the observation booth, which is at the rear of the classroom. The stimulating effects of parts of this room will be apparent in the use of open shelves, exposed materials, reading charts, and other equipment not in immediate use. It should be understood, however, that these photographs were taken at the end of several years of room utilization, when many of the children no longer needed learning environments which were as completely stimulus-free as had earlier been the case.

building because of space needs. The principal of this school had not attended the administrators' seminar. T–45 feels rather alone in this building, and further feels that she does not have the status here that she had in her previous school. She reports that her former principal, who had attended the seminar, was supportive of her program and very helpful, but the present principal knows nothing about the program and has not been very supportive. During the site visit T–45, speaking in a very quiet tone, constantly gestured or talked to individual children to keep them quiet (see interaction analysis).

T–45 reported that she does not have the support or supplies she needs for her program. Many of her pupils are receiving outside services from other specialists, leading her to comment that at times her room

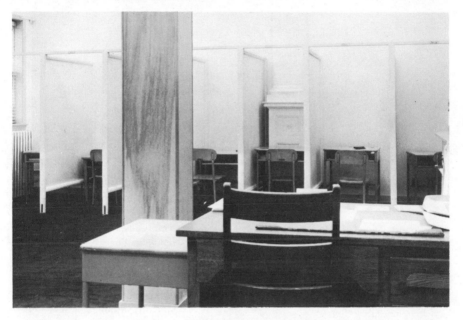

Figure 23. The cubicle area. This section of the classroom follows general project recommendations almost as closely as the original design of the room has allowed. The exposed radiator and the venetian blind are obvious distractors, but this section of the room is relatively stimulus-free.

is like "Grand Central Station." In reply to a benign comment about the behavior of the children, T–45 responded, "You should know that we were really performing for you today and on our best behavior."

These two teachers tended to accept rather passively the administrative decisions, supply situations, and class sizes. They were generally "left alone" by the system's program coordinator.

Several other teachers in the same system eventually incurred the coordinator's wrath. These were individuals who were highly motivated and knew what was needed for their classes, but who lacked the maturity, experience, and skills necessary to "get from the system" those things and conditions which were necessary for

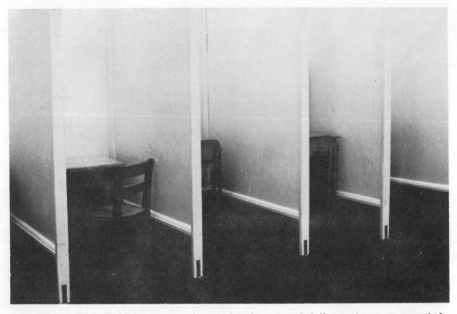

Figure 24. Cubicle construction which in general follows the recommended form. Note, however, the movable furniture, particularly the desks which will serve as distractors to some children. Note also the small cracks in the vertical molding of the center cubicle. These are large enough for a child to insert his pencil point and they will serve as a distractor to children who are characterized by motor disinhibition. The space at the bottom, large enough for children to get their feet and hands under, will also serve as a distractor, although it was probably recommended as an aid to janitorial personnel for cleaning purposes. Building and ground needs should not be paramount to educational and psychological needs of these children.

the successful implementation of their programs. These teachers eventually became so discouraged that they left after one year.

The program coordinator was highly critical of T–38's performance in the classroom since her return from the training project. He felt her performance was an indication of the invalidity of the training project's approach to dealing with these kinds of children. He further felt that T–38 had "forgotten everything she ever knew" about grouping children for instruction. He remarked that individual teaching of the type T–38 wanted to carry on could not be done in this type of classroom situation. At this time he stated that, of all the teachers in his program, not one of those who had attended the training project was considered by him to be among the best.

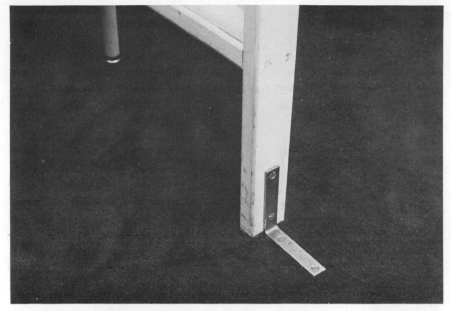

Figure 25. Detail showing floor fixture of cubicles shown in Figure 24. A better arrangement of the angle bracket would have been to install it on the interior side of the upright prior to the installation of carpeting. In this manner its stimulus value would be further reduced.

Although T–38's principal had attended the administrators' seminar, this person reflected views similar to those of the coordinator insofar as they related to "grouping" for instruction. He acknowledged the logistical deficiencies associated with T–38's classroom and frankly divorced himself from any attempts to "fight the system" (sic) for those things which the teacher felt were essential to the program.

Neither of the other two systems had curriculum or supervisory services for their programs dealing with brain-injured children. In each case the teachers, although reporting to a central system agency, were immediately responsible to, and had to rely entirely upon their principals for program support and administrative guidance.

In most respects T–48's first post-training year was a satisfying one. She returned to a school which contained other well-established special classes and a strong principal who had attended the administrators' seminar. T–48's self-concepts were somewhat inadequate insofar as they pertained to her ability to manage pupil behavior. This teacher felt constantly threatened by a self-perceived inability to control the actions of her pupils. Though she was far from the most skilled or experienced teacher in the training group she was, in the opinions of both project personnel and her principal, much more capable than she credited herself as being. Though T–48 had not been involved in the pupil selection process, the

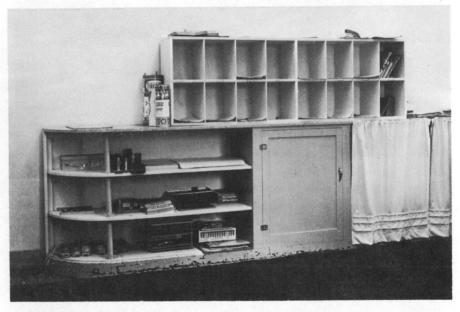

Figure 26. Open storage areas together with exposed materials add to the distractions with which children must cope.

children in the class had been appropriately identified and met project criteria. Although much of the first year was spent by teacher and principal in solving logistical problems, resulting in an almost constant state of flux in daily classroom life, it was the consensus of principal, school psychologist, and project personnel that the pupils had demonstrated marked gains by the end of the year. This success was in part attributable to the school principal, who had been able to communicate to the other teachers the nature of T–48's program, and who had further been able to provide T–48 with firm support in her relationships with other teachers, parents, and the central administration. At the end of the first year, the principal was promoted to a post in the central administration.

The replacement principal had not, of course, attended the administrators' seminar. Neither did this individual possess any background of experience or training in any field of special education. Upon assuming his new position this principal was immediately confronted with a host of problems stemming from a

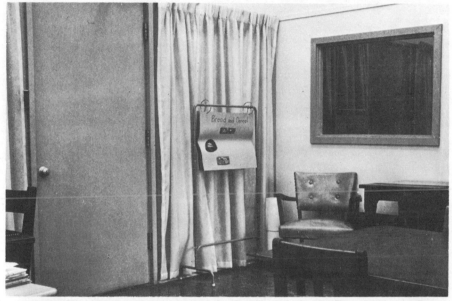

Figure 27.   The one-way observation window and the reading chart are obvious distractors here. Note the drapes used to cover floor-to-ceiling windows. While the school system agreed to the major interior modifications necessary for the construction of an observation booth and window, it was unwilling to paint over these large windows which looked out on a corridor.

school population which was rapidly changing in its basic characteristics, and increasing in size. In view of these problems, this principal felt himself unable to either justify using classrooms for smaller-than-average groups of children, or to devote the time necessary to keep the classroom of a relatively "weak" teacher operating effectively. He had, accordingly, set in motion a chain of events which eventually led to removing most of the special classes from his building. At the time of the final on-site visit, plans were afoot for the removal of T–48's class from that school. Noth-

Figure 28. This almost conventional-looking work area was at the opposite end of the room depicted in Figure 27. Here pupils who no longer needed complete space and stimulus control were able to work singly and in small groups, in preparation for regular class integration.

ing was known as to its anticipated location—only that it would be taken out of that school.

Without the support of the former principal, T–48 perceived herself as completely unable to manage her class effectively. She was so threatened in this respect that she invested as much—if not more—energy in reacting to these anxieties as she did in managing her classroom. During successive site visits there were succeedingly fewer evidences of project rationale or methods present in her classroom or in her program.

T–30 (upon returning to another system) was given an opportunity to review work-up information relating to candidates for her prospective class. She was further allowed to participate in final placement decisions. When school opened in September, the teacher was allowed to build her class membership at her own speed. This was accomplished in spite of parental pressures for immediate admittance. These pressures had been transmitted through upper echelon administrators in the direction of the teacher, but had been intercepted by the school principal.

The principal, who had attended the administrators' seminar, acted as a constant buffer between outside pressures such as these, and the teacher was allowed to operate her class on a half-day basis for as long as she deemed necessary. The principal remained intimately connected with the program and was almost always immediately available to the teacher. He took active steps to orient other teachers in the school to the characteristics and goals of the teacher's program. The teacher had a record of highly successful elementary school teaching experience. She was adequately supplied, her classroom was appropriately modified, and she had the services of a full-time assistant.

During her first post-training year she experienced many organizational and management problems within her classroom (see interaction analysis). These were only very slowly resolved, mainly through the availability of the school principal. With understandings gained through the seminar and his own further reading, the principal felt secure enough to give the teacher specific support and tentative advice in dealing with her behavioral management problems. Toward the end of the first year, when pressures for reintegration were forthcoming, the principal again interposed himself between the pressure sources and the teacher. By the middle of the second year the teacher was established firmly enough so that much of the principal's support was no longer necessary.

For some rather obvious reasons, it appears that the most significant system contacts these returning teachers had were with the principals of the schools in which their classrooms were located.

As teachers differed in their technical, and interpersonal skills, and in their motivation, so did the principals. Various combinations of teachers and principals with varying sets of these characteristics resulted in cases where some strong teachers were further strengthened, but where others were forced to dissipate their energies in fighting their systems. Other combinations produced situations where weaker teachers were either strengthened or rendered completely ineffective by the principals with whom they came into contact.

DIFFERENCES WITHIN A SINGLE SYSTEM

Two teachers sent by the same system (in different years) were successful in establishing programs for different sets of reasons.

Both T–17 and T–33 had been sent to the Syracuse training project upon the recommendation of the same administrator. T–33, upon returning, was placed directly within that administrator's department. The class to which T–17 was assigned, on the other hand, fell in another department, which was partially affected by non-system funding. Although the administrator had curriculum and instructional-supervisory responsibilities for T–17's program, he had no administrative authority whatsoever in connection with it. All decisions affecting the class were made by administrators in the other department, without—in the estimation of project personnel—concomitant responsibilities for the efficacy of the program in the class.

It eventually became apparent that the administrator originally alluded to, already heavily overextended in supervisory commitments, was not as closely involved with T–17's program as he was with T–33's. This was construed by project personnel as a major reason for a very hectic first post-training year for T–17.

During T–33's training year the department administrator, rather than a principal, attended the administrators' seminar, as the location of the classroom-to-be had not at that time been determined. The attending administrator had been instrumental in selecting T–33 for the training project. When the classroom's location was finally decided upon, this administrator actively pursued the activities necessary for appropriately modifying and supplying the room and for providing the teacher with a full-time assistant. In spite of the large size of the school system and a shortage of supervisory staff, the administrator took a close personal interest in the progress of T–33's class. This person was responsible for opening channels and establishing many precedents for the extra-classroom involvement of the classroom teacher in matters affecting her class.

T–33's principal was an educator with a wide and long-established reputation for successful educational innovation. Possessing little specific information about the nature of T–33's program at the start, this principal provided T–33 not only with the necessary housekeeping support, but also with a working milieu receptive to new educational ideas. Within a very short time T–33, in addition to her own class, was working informally with children from some of the regular classrooms in that school. She was also used as a resource person by many of the teachers. One site visit occurred during a period when T–33 was involved either full-time or part-time with fifteen pupils.

The program operated by T–33 eventually became one in which the system took considerable satisfaction and pride. In addition to its basic purpose, it was used as a practicum facility for student teachers under the supervision of T–33. Equipped with an observation booth, it was frequently visited by individuals and groups from universities, state education departments, and members of other school systems.

The school in which T–33 was located eventually received a new principal, one who proved to be generally unsympathetic to any activity which threatened to interfere with either the smooth operation of the building or (as perceived by him) its educational program. This principal made some early, arbitrary decisions which rather seriously affected some of the latitude within which T–33 had been allowed to operate.

By that time, the system had developed such a deep commitment to T–33's program that when news of these decisions, and T–33's dissatisfaction with them, filtered up through the hierarchy, word was received by the principal from the very highest system levels to the effect that continued friction of that type would place his own position in jeopardy.

Shortly after this situation was resolved, T–33 received a supervisory appointment in the system's department of special education.

T–17 was assigned to teach a class of socially maladjusted children in an inner-city elementary school in the same city. The class had been in existence for a year, and T–17's predecessor had figured significantly in the pupil selection process. The previous teacher was described by system personnel as having conceptualized the teacher role as one of a therapist rather than as primarily that of an educator. Ostensibly, this teacher had selected pupils deemed amenable to whatever therapy she considered herself equipped to administer. When T–17 took over, those pupils who had not been excluded during the previous year were present in the classroom.

The class is located in the cellar of the building. This is not to be confused with "ground floor," or "basement"—this room is in the cellar. The classroom's windows, approximately two feet high and three feet wide, are in the top right-hand corner of the wall facing the entrance door. During most of the site visit the classroom was filled with the noises of trash can bottoms being dragged past the windows. The classroom wall into which these windows were set was a maze of asbestos-covered steam pipes stretching from wall to wall and from floor to ceiling. During each of two site visits, very little instruction took place, as teacher and assistant were busy controlling the behavior of the class members. During one visit, the assistant principal was called in twice to temporarily remove recalcitrant pupils.

The principal had not attended the administrators' seminar. This individual was perceived by all concerned (including project personnel) as an effective administrator in an extremely difficult school, performing in a manner satisfactory to the system administration, the school staff, and most of the parents of the children in the school.

When queried about the composition of T–17's class, the principal explained that this was a class that had received a new teacher, just as any class might at the beginning of a new school year. Though expressing doubt as to the efficacy of the special class model as an intervention technique, the principal expressed the intention of supporting the teacher. He further stated that in the future, when children were considered for placement in the class, T–17 would be given final decision-making authority. T–17 spent the remainder of the year in that teaching situation. Somewhat to the surprise of project personnel, she returned to the same teaching assignment the following year.

The entire membership of last year's class has been sent back to regular classes in that school building. They still receive certain supportive services from T–17, but are officially assigned to regular grades. It was reported that by the spring semester of last year the pupils were spending from one half to two thirds of their time in regular classrooms in preparation for full reintegration. T–17 reports resistance and resentment from the "regular" teachers in the school, further reporting a general unwillingness on their part to admit that many of the children who had always been in their classrooms were functioning at academic and behavioral levels no different than those of the reintegrated pupils. In an attempt to reduce some of this hostility, T–17 has been "taking" the reintegrated group for lunch thus far this year, and will continue to do so until she has built up her new class to near its full complement. In addition she has been working informally with individual pupils from regular classes. The school principal has lived up to his statements of last year relative to the teacher's final decision-making authority. T–17 reports that she has had opportunities to observe all of the incoming pupils in their present classrooms, and was given prerogatives of acceptance or rejection in each case. The classroom is still in its cellar location although plans have been announced to move it upstairs when some (anticipated) space is available. The classroom is now adequately furnished and equipped.

T–17 somehow survived the first post-training year in an all-but-impossible teaching situation. She not only survived, but managed to "clean house," and opted to return the following year, building an entirely new class centered around children she felt competent to deal with.

HOW TWO PROGRAMS WERE ESTABLISHED

As was the case with T–17, T–12 was assigned to an "emotionally disturbed" class by her school system in her first post-training year.

During the course of that year she became aware of the existence of numbers of children who fitted almost classical descriptions of the psychopathology attributed to brain-injured children. Convinced of the need for an educational program for these children, especially those at early school ages, she discussed this in detail with the system's supervisor of special education. These two people then took steps to bring this need to the attention of the administration, and went on to outline the philosophy, rationale, and pupil inclusion criteria for such a program. A class was opened the following September, with T–12 as its teacher. The usual problems of intrasystem communication difficulties and cliche-criticisms (e.g., "She has only six or eight pupils, yet wants to place them in *our* classrooms!") were present at that time, and still exist to some degree.

A referral-evaluation-placement operation was worked out that included T–12 as an essential element. The school day of the special class ends at 1:30 P.M.

When a child is under consideration for placement in the class, T–12 observes the child in his present classroom. This is accomplished by T–12 dashing from her building at 1:30 over to the school in which the child is presently attending class. This may be done on one or more days. T–12 then describes the child's behavior and relates it to the potential her program has for modifying it. T–12's reports are full of cogent descriptive information and do not hesitate to make specific recommendations either for inclusion or exclusion from her program.

The transition procedure stipulates that at the outset of reintegration, the children are dismissed from regular class attendance early in the afternoon, to receive homebound instruction designed to reduce any academic deficiencies which may be operating to inhibit success in the new classroom. Each child receives five hours of homebound instruction per week.

T–12 did not have a teacher assistant, but at various times she had personally obtained the services of a Red Cross volunteer. Several of the children's parents were in the habit of coming in at varying intervals to render what assistance they could. Several fathers had been helpful in making or modifying classroom furniture. Some had reproduced, at their own expense, either instructional materials or information designed for dissemination to the other parents.

T–12 reported that she had been quite active with the parents of her pupils, meeting with them as a group once a month, in addition to scheduling individual conferences during each month. She feels that, in addition to satisfying many of their information needs, she had been able to convey some understanding of her program goals and the relationships between specifics of the program and these goals.

System personnel report that T–12 has been active in communicating information about her program to others interested in learning problems of children. She has spoken at teachers' meetings and has been available for after-school consultation. She has been especially effective with the teachers of two "learning impairments" classes located in her school building. Over the course of two years, she has spared no effort in complying with their requests for information and counsel. In her estimation, and in that of the principal, the two teachers are now doing high quality work. T–12 emphasizes, however, that they were excellent teachers to begin with.

T–12's program contained many ingredients necessary to its success. Definite administrative commitment appeared to exist in terms of servicing the pupils in the program, who in turn satisfied a specifically articulated set of inclusion criteria. Adequate support in the form of physical facilities, supplies, and equipment had been forthcoming, though the very necessary aide had not. The teacher's own knowledge of the type of pupil best served by the program she was prepared to offer, coupled with the understanding and leadership of local supervisory personnel, had offset problems presented by less than fully adequate diagnostic services to a considerable degree. The teacher had demonstrated a mature competence in dealing with other system personnel and with adults in the community. She had taken steps to communicate with parents to such an extent that parents seek her out, visit her classroom freely, contribute time and materials, meet with her periodically, and attempt to provide at-home reinforcement of concepts, attitudes, and skills presented in the classroom.

Both T–12 and T–17 succeeded in establishing project-type programs during their second post-training years. Each, upon returning from the training project, had been assigned to existent special classes for heterogeneous groups of behaviorally deviant children.

Because of maturity, experience, and long acquaintance with many of the school district's power figures, T–12 was able to utilize a well-rounded approach to the establishment of a program for brain-injured children. Through T–12 and several special education administrators, the entire system was sensitized to a need and steps were taken to satisfy it.

T–17, on the other hand, was a young teacher in a very large system, able to communicate only with those immediately contiguous with her classroom (principal, psychologist). T–17's program was established on a molecular level, almost entirely from elements already present in the school building to which the class was assigned. With the help of a strong principal T–17 was able, in spite of considerable teacher resistance, to reintegrate all of the first-year pupils back into regular classes by the end of that year. This was not accomplished by administrative fiat alone. T–17 worked hard, not only to prepare the pupils for reintegration, but also to maintain them in their new classes during the first months of the following year.

T–12 and T–17, with different armamentariums of resources, each capitalized fully on what was available to them.

WIIO DESIGNS LOCAL PROGRAMS?

Some program administrators—especially those in small or middle-sized school districts—were without extensive backgrounds of training or experience relating to the educational problems of exceptional children. They had, however, become aware of an acute (though nonspecific) need for dealing with certain pupils who, though not necessarily mentally retarded, were not profiting from regular classroom instruction: children who all too frequently were disruptive elements in these regular classrooms. When these administrators heard of the existence of a funded training program at the university level, and when they were able to send a teacher to that program, they felt—rightfully—that they had taken a concrete step in addressing that need.

Either the administrators themselves, or the appropriate school principals, attended the administrators' seminar, receiving short but intensive exposure to the rationale and specifics of the project-recommended approach to dealing educationally with brain-injured children. For many of them, this was the first direct professional contact with any organized body of information dealing with behaviorally deviant children. When the classes opened in the fall, many of the administrators and their systems looked upon the teachers as the "experts," and proceeded to wait for positive results. The fact that in most instances these results were soon forthcoming is presented at this point as only incidental to the situation to be described next.

T–18 and T–23 returned to school systems which had many characteristics in common. Neither system had ever had a class for behaviorally deviant children of any type. When decisions were made to establish such classes upon the return of the teachers, both were placed under their systems' chief pupil personnel services administrators. The professional backgrounds of the two administrators were similar in that both had functioned as guidance personnel, and had little first-hand knowledge of either special education in general or the education of emotionally disturbed or brain-injured children in particular. Both had attended the administrators' seminar, not knowing at that time who the teachers' principals were to be. Both appeared to be extremely receptive to the information presented at the seminar and eventually developed some understanding of the nature of the project-type program. Both worked very closely with their teachers in planning for the new programs. In each case, the teachers were viewed both as primary information sources and as final decision-making figures on matters pertaining to the programs. Both administrators were able to secure whatever funds and resources were requested by the teachers for modifying, equipping, and supplying the new classrooms. Both classes were placed in modern elementary school buildings in suburban-rural settings, under very cooperative principals who had never dealt with special education programs of any type.

The cooperative attitudes displayed by these principals might more accurately have been described as passive, in a positive sense. Both made every effort to comply with teacher and system requests but did not themselves develop or adopt positions or concepts relating to the programs. Both appeared to perceive the programs in their buildings as surrounded by a somewhat impenetrable mystique.

The system which sent T–18 to the training project had been sensitized to the need of special classes for emotionally disturbed children through an extensive report compiled by the area's leading medical, psychiatric, and mental health authorities and published by the county mental health association. After hearing of the training project from the project director, a top-echelon system administrator selected T–18 for training.

T–23's attendance at the training project was self-initiated. After hearing about the training project from the teacher, the system agreed to enter into the necessary commitments.

The administrators in both school systems were enthusiastically supportive of the new programs and made it clear that more classes of the same type were needed. Project personnel received the impression that classes for brain-injured children were viewed by the local administrators as the answer to the problems of emotionally disturbed children, and therefore felt it necessary at one point to suggest that other intervention models existed that would be more appropriate for many other children.

T–18's system was convinced that more classes of the same type were needed. Funds were located enabling the system to send teachers to a full year of post-graduate study on full salary and with all expenses paid. A system announcement to this effect, designed to solicit applicants, received no response. Several teachers were found who agreed to attend summer courses at nearby universities with programs in emotional disturbance.

Special classes were opened with these teachers in the fall. Their course work and training had no connection, of course, with the rationale of the Syracuse training project. By this time, T–18 had accepted a position outside of the system, and her modified classroom was closed.

T–23 and her administrator very early became active in recruiting more teachers for the following year. Several were located and placed, receiving in-service training by T–23.

In both of these school systems the project teachers were the main—if not sole—bases upon which their programs rested. While the systems were sympathetic, supportive, and even enthusiastic in helping the teachers establish the new programs, the system administrators had never acquired the insights necessary to either accept or reject the programs on the basis of their rationale. When the programs were successful, these administrators were delighted and immediately looked to expanding them. Little awareness was evidenced of the existence of other types of disturbed children in their districts who were in need of other types of programs.

After T–18 left her system, and when the summer-trained teachers returned, few signs of the type of program initiated by T–18 remained.

The program in T–23's system appears at this writing to be assured of somewhat longer life—as long as T–23 remains with the system. If T–23 were to leave, however, the program would soon lose its unique identity regardless of the presence of other teachers who had received in-service training. No power figures in the system have developed any important insights into the program beyond the fact that "it works."

Nothing is known by project personnel of the quality of the new programs in T–18's system, nor of the quality of the new teachers in T–23's program, but that is not the point being made here. The point is that these systems were typical of some others in that a general lack of broad and specific understandings of the educational needs of large groups of children was so widespread that many systems were unable to plan programs—and indeed were unaware of alternatives to be considered—but rather were at the mercy of the teacher supply, and had only been able at best to locate teachers with certain suspected competencies, leaving the actual design of the programs to the teachers themselves.

WHY WERE THEY SENT?

Another group of school systems did not see fit to use their returning teachers with brain-injured children.

T–07 was assigned to a class of hyperaggressive mentally retarded children. The principal of the building to which the class was assigned had no direct connection with the class, and was uninterested in talking with project personnel. The supervisor who had attended the administrators' seminar reported having spent a great deal of time with T–07 relative to problems the teacher was experiencing in instruction and management with—as reported by the supervisor—few apparent results. T–07 was totally uninvolved in placement staffing, nor was ready access to diagnostic staff available. Though classes for brain-injured children existed within the system, it was made clear that personnel connected with these classes had refused to consider employing T–07 in this program when the teacher's return from training was imminent. Upper-echelon administrators in the system voiced extreme discontent with T–07 and indicated that the teacher would not be asked to return the following year. When questioned as to why the teacher, a veteran of that system, had been selected and sent to the Syracuse training program, the reply was that it was hoped such training would improve the teacher's attitudes and abilities, and that such an appointment would get the teacher "out of the way" for a year. The principal with whom T–07 worked prior to project attendance expressed complete ignorance as to how or why the teacher had been selected by the system for attendance in the project. This principal did not remember writing any letter of recommendation. The frankly reported reaction of this person upon learning of T–07's appointment to the Syracuse training project was: "Forty master's degrees will not make [T–07] an efficient teacher."

T–24 was employed in a vaguely defined role sometimes described as fitting a "crisis teacher" model. In a description of this teacher's program, written by the teacher, students from regular classes were to report to T–25 both regularly for scheduled periods of instruction and at those times when emotionally loaded incidents appeared to be brewing in the regular classrooms. T–25's first post-training principal said that in the fall, on very short notice, he had been informed that a new program was to be placed in his building. He reports that children were then hurriedly selected from classes in the building, and the program was started. He said that it was his impression that the program was based on the teaching monograph (Cruickshank, *et al.*), upon which his elbow rested throughout the conference. He had not attended the administrators' seminar, and expressed his disappointment at this fact.

During each of a number of site-visits by project personnel it became apparent that T–25 was seeing very few children in the course of a typical school day. Most of the teacher's time was spent moving about the building chatting with whoever was found to be free, or in the "crisis" classroom alone. These impressions were eventually confirmed by system administrators, and a subsequently appointed principal. When this issue was raised in a session with system administrators, these individuals replied that the system had been aware of the situation for some time, and had plans for employing this teacher in a different role in the following year.

T–04 was never employed in a project context. Upon returning, she was assigned to a class of emotionally disturbed adolescents. At the end of the first post-training year she returned to a pre-training elementary school teaching assignment.

T–04 had taught an elementary grade prior to entering the training project. The principal with whom she worked described her as an excellent and enthusiastic teacher, but also as one who engendered numerous complaints from parents because of involving her classes in "controversial" discussions. The principal reported that T–04 never asked for outside help, but always insisted on solving her own problems in her own ways. According to the principal T–04 never appeared to have shown a great deal of interest in children with learning problems, but did address a great deal of effort to the more gifted members of her classes. When T–04 applied to the system for admittance to the training project the principal supplied the system with a positive letter of recommendation.

The psychologist connected with the program in which T–04 was teaching was most enthusiastic about her in an interview with project personnel in the early fall of the first year. In a second interview held toward the end of the same school year the same psychologist described T–04 as a very rigid person, one who had to feel absolute confidence in her own absolute ability to work with any children assigned to her. He reported that T–04 at all times considered herself to be the sole dictator of classroom policy, feeling that she was the only person able to provide information relative to the behavioral dynamics of her pupils. She was in continual conflict with her building principal, with any other perceived authority figures, and many teachers as well. T–04 saw herself as the only person to whom her pupils could relate in any meaningful way. The psychologist felt that the classroom milieu created by T–04 was rather Darwinian in nature, with constant emphasis on inter-pupil competition. Although the psychologist felt that some of the pupils may have benefitted from this type of environmental press, he was sure that others had not.

When interviewed in the fall of the first year, the principal of the school in which T–04's class was located reported that he had been impressed with T–04's credentials and had welcomed her arrival, but had rather quickly developed doubts about the teacher's stated classroom goals. The principal was confessedly academic-oriented, while the teacher's orientation was expressed more in terms of behavioral changes. The principal later rated T–04 negatively in almost every area of functioning.

SUCCESS IN SPITE OF THE SYSTEM

A few administrators proved to be somewhat apathetic about establishing programs which would make effective use of their project-trained teachers. Rather than as a corollary to differing or opposing education viewpoints, this apathy was most frequently manifested as a result of feeling threatened by a system commitment which made demands on these individuals that had never been made before. The commitment to establish classes for brain-injured children made it necessary for these administrators to take the initiative in obtaining heavy allotments of system resources; in establishing new or additional channels of intrasystem communication; in informing or persuading others in the system to cooperate; and in becoming familiar with a new (to them) body of information. As tentative efforts to meet these demands met resistance, many succumbed, rationalizing either in terms of the inappropriateness of the project model or in terms of the absence of pupils who met criteria.

With this state of affairs existing as frequently as it did, project personnel were not overly surprised at finding in some teachers' classes many pupils who did not meet criteria. What *was* surprising was the fact that so many of these pupils subsequently appeared to respond positively to such placement.

T–05's director of special education had attended the administrators' seminar.

T–05 had no connection with her new class until it opened in the fall. The classroom had for the most part been appropriately modified. T–05 had not been involved in any phase of the pupil selection process. The pupils reflected little in the way of project criteria, but had in common only histories of unacceptable classroom behavior—most of it violent. The group included several who had been diagnosed as mentally retarded by system psychologists.

Pupil service personnel appeared to know little of either the rationale for dealing with brain-injured children or the behavioral signs to look for in identifying them.

Partly due to an unscheduled visit to the classroom by a group of administrators who had not been prepared for the physical modifications they were to see, certain misconceptions about the program quickly spread throughout the system, causing other teachers to become extremely reluctant in referring any of their pupils for placement in it. These misconceptions were only dealt with passively by the administrators connected with the program. A single exception here was T–05's principal who, while not having attended the seminar, rendered invaluable support within the school building.

After a few frustrating weeks, the teacher realized that a program for brain-injured children would be inappropriate for most of the class members, and began changing the nature of her educational planning.

By the middle of the second post-training year the pupils had demonstrated remarkable behavioral and academic gains (confirmed by the school principal).

After the original visitor-fiasco T–05 had become hypersensitive to any possible effects visitors may have had on the class members, and had accordingly adopted a rather hostile attitude to the presence of outsiders in the classroom. This issue was also dealt with passively by the program administrators, with the result that almost no one ever ventured into the room.

As a result of this self-imposed and administratively-condoned isolation, the gains made by the pupils largely went unrecognized, and the original misconceptions about the program took a long time in dying— and were not yet dead at the time of the final on-site visit.

TEACHER-PUPIL INTERACTION

In the final two years of the project follow-up phase, the Flanders System of Classroom Interaction Analysis [9] was introduced as a framework for describing the social-emotional climates of the classrooms operated by the project teachers. This system is designed to produce a record of teacher-pupil interactions conceptualized around the teacher's control of the students' freedom of action. Analysis of such records enables the investigator to distinguish between the acts of the teacher which increase and those which limit freedom of action on the part of pupils.

The categories of teacher-pupil interaction are listed in the following chart. Seven of the categories describe talk by the teacher. Two describe talk by the pupil. The tenth is a general category for periods of "silence or confusion." The seven teacher-talk categories represent both indirect and direct verbalisms employed by the teacher in the attempt to reach whatever program goals have been stipulated for the pupils in the class. Categories one through four represent indirect influence, while five, six, and seven reflect direct influence.

After becoming thoroughly familiar with the categories and the ground rules for assigning them to observed interaction, the observer is able to sit in the classroom and record a category number approximately every three seconds. In this way, a record is kept of the teacher-pupil interactions taking place during the observation period and the resulting raw data can be analyzed sequentially. As it is known that a category was recorded approximately every three seconds it is possible to see how long each one

CATEGORIES FOR INTERACTION ANALYSIS[†]

TEACHER TALK		STUDENT TALK
Indirect Influence	Direct Influence	
1.* ACCEPTS FEELINGS: accepts and clarifies the tone of feeling of the students in an unthreatening manner. Feelings may be positive or negative. Predicting or recalling feelings are included.	5.* LECTURING: giving facts or opinions about content or procedure; expressing his own ideas, asking rhetorical questions.	8.* STUDENT TALK—RESPONSE: talk by students in response to teacher. Teacher initiates the contact or solicits student statement.
2.* PRAISES OR ENCOURAGES: praises or encourages student action or behavior. Jokes that release tension, but not at the expense of another individual, nodding head or saying "umhm?" or "go on" are included.	6.* GIVING DIRECTIONS: directions, commands, or orders which students are expected to comply with.	9.* STUDENT TALK—INITIATION: talk initiated by students. If "calling on" student is only to indicate who may talk next, observer must decide whether student wanted to talk.
3.* ACCEPTS OR USES IDEAS OF STUDENT: clarifying, building, or developing ideas suggested by a student. As teacher brings more of his own ideas into play, shift to category 5.	7.* CRITICIZING OR JUSTIFYING AUTHORITY: statements intended to change student behavior from unacceptable to acceptable pattern; bawling someone out; stating why the teacher is doing what he is doing; extreme self-reference.	
4.* ASKS QUESTIONS: asking a question about content or procedure with the intent that a student answer.		

10.* SILENCE OR CONFUSION: pauses, short periods of silence and periods of confusion in which communication cannot be understood by the observer.

* There is NO scale implied by these numbers. Each number is classificatory, designating a particular kind of communication event. To write these numbers down during observation is merely to identify and enumerate communication events, not to judge them.

† Flanders, *Teacher Influence, Pupil Attitudes, and Achievement*, p. 20.

lasted, what preceded it, and what followed it. Thus the observer leaves the classroom with a record of what—in an operationally defined sense— happened while he was there.

The data can be analyzed in another dimension by entering it in a matrix consisting of equal numbers of category columns and rows (see following pages). The cells of the matrix are defined by reading first the row number, then the column number. The data is entered by making tally marks in the appropriate cells for sequential pairs of numbers, using each number twice, first as a row designator and next as a column designator. As an example, for the raw data, 10 6 9 3 5 4 8 9, the cell entries would be 10–6, 6–9, 9–3, 3–5, 5–4, 4–8, and 8–9. It is then possible to convert column totals to percentages of the whole, allowing the reader to learn the relative percentages of time in which each type of interaction took place, as well as percentages of time in which teachers talked and pupils talked. For further information on the process and analysis of teacher-pupil interaction, the reader is referred to the previously cited reference [10].

Flanders' "indirect-direct" dichotomy is value-oriented toward the "indirect" dimensions. For example, "Indirect influence encourages student participation and thereby increases his freedom of action. . . . Direct influence increases the active control of the teacher and often stimulates conformity and compliance" [11]. Research with normal pupils in elementary and secondary grades reported upon by that writer [12] and others [13] tentatively appears to support this orientation.

While the project rationale would alter the direction of this value orientation to a certain extent, it would do so only in the context of attempting to bring extremely disorganized individuals into focus with their environments so that they may eventually become stimulus-discriminant to the extent that they are able to relate in mutually satisfying fashions to public school teachers and all other elements of society.

In terms of the project rationale, a direct teacher is one who is able to exercise such total control over pupils' environments and actions that she is able to introduce additional and different elements into these spheres as pupils gain in their abilities to deal effectively with them. The project teacher is one who has as an ultimate goal an effective, nondirective relationship with the student, but who at the same time is capable of assuming the role of an extremely directive person when the situation demands it—and this demand is an exceedingly heavy one indeed during the early stages of programming.

Directiveness, as used here, is by no means to be confused with either rigidity or dogmatism [14]. Neither single beliefs nor systems of beliefs should have been overly resistant to change on the part of the project teacher. As used in the context of teaching brain-injured children, directiveness refers to the ability of the teacher to totally structure the psychological and physical environments and implement an educational program within them. Effective implementation demands that the teacher be constantly attuned to changes in pupil cognition, affect, and behavior, and be prepared to alter or modify the program instantaneously so as to optimally cope with such change.

Flanders makes use of the ratio between indirect and direct teacher verbalisms as a measure of teacher influence [15]. At least two of these indirect-direct ratios are in use, the numerators and denominators of each consisting of different combinations of category totals. The "big" I/D ratio is computed by dividing the totals of categories 1, 2, 3, and 4, by the totals of categories 5, 6, and 7. The "small" i/d will be used for descriptive purposes in this section of the report. It is computed by dividing the totals of categories 1, 2, and 3, by the totals of categories 6 and 7. Flanders states that, "The i/d ratio is considered to be less influenced by the nature of the content being taught [than is the big I/D ratio] [16]." This becomes apparent when it is known that the first three categories are defined by affective and supportive statements, and categories 6 and 7 pertain to directions and criticisms by the teacher.

The mechanics of recording verbal interaction require the observer to be physically situated where he can see and hear what takes place between the teacher and her pupils. Such was not always possible during the site visits. Of the 37 teachers who taught brain-injured children during the four-year post-training follow-up period, only 12 had classrooms which were equipped with observation booths. Three of the booths were furnished with auditory amplification equipment while the others were not. It was necessary for the observers to sit in the classroom proper in most cases, but even when doing this it was not possible to hear what teachers and pupils said in every case. The construction of cubicles in some of the rooms actually masked sounds to the extent that teacher-pupil interchanges could not be heard by an observer sitting a few feet away. Interaction recording was not accomplished in these classrooms, nor was it attempted with a teacher who only had two children in her room at the time of the site visit. Interaction records were made in 30 of the 37 classrooms.

All but three of these records were compiled by the same project observer. The other three were compiled by another observer; only one of them will be presented in this report, together with instructions to regard it cautiously when comparing it to the other records. The reason for this is that an earlier computation of a Scott Coefficient [17] produced an index of inter-observer agreement only to the magnitude of 0.60.

Another reason exists for regarding the interaction information in this report with some degree of caution. In attempts to make themselves as inconspicuous as possible (to both pupils and teachers) the observers did not use stop watches to time their recording. Timing was done by glancing surreptitiously at the rather tiny second hands of their wristwatches. It was determined that this *modus operandi* introduced possible errors of up to 20 seconds in some of the recording sessions.

The actual recording of classroom interaction was done during periods when individualized instruction was taking place. Though such periods occurred throughout the day in each classroom, only sessions which were scheduled in the morning will be reported upon here.

Pupils were seated at their desks during these individualized instructional periods, with the teacher moving from pupil to pupil, either checking work or performing instruction.

CROSS-SECTIONAL INFORMATION

On a cross-sectional basis, when the i/d ratios of 17 teachers who had been in their first year of teaching brain-injured children were compared with those of 13 teachers who had taught brain-injured children for two or more years, the mean i/d ratios of 0.77 and 0.57 respectively yielded a *t* value of 0.951, which was non-significant.

CASE STUDY INFORMATION

Four teachers who returned to the same system were mentioned earlier in this chapter. All returned in the same year. Two were described as aggressive in soliciting system logistical support, and two were described as passive in this respect.

Table VIII summarizes in percentage form the interaction

TABLE VIII

CLASSROOM INTERACTION SAMPLES FOR FOUR TEACHERS
WHO RETURNED TO THE SAME SYSTEM*

| | TEACHER | | | |
| | Aggressive | | Passive | |
	T–32	T–39	T–10	T–45
TEACHER TALK				
(1) Affect	0	3	†	1
(2) Praise	2	5	1	2
(3) Accepts	1	5	2	2
(4) Questions	7	17	15	6
(5) Lectures	18	16	12	1
(6) Directs	2	11	14	13
(7) Criticizes	0	4	1	16
Total Teacher Talk	30	61	45	41
PUPIL TALK				
(8) Response	53	26	10	14
(9) Initiated	1	10	6	8
Total Pupil Talk	54	36	16	22
(10) Silence, Confusion	16	3	39	37

* All figures are percentages.
† < 1 per cent.

which took place in the four teachers' classrooms during periods which were recorded by the same observer in a single week.

The classrooms of the aggressive teachers saw pupils responding to the teachers (Category 8) 63 per cent and 26 per cent of the time, respectively. In the classrooms of the passive teachers, these figures were 10 per cent and 14 per cent. In view of the fact that per cents of time spent in asking questions were similar (Category 4: 7, 17, and 15, 6) a question may be directed to the markedly less frequent occurrence of pupil responses in the classrooms of the passive teachers.

T–10's interaction matrix (see Figure 29) shows that most of her questions which were not followed by pupil responses (4–8) were actually followed by silence or confusion (4–10). The matrix

Teacher 32 Time: 9:20 - 9:39

Category	Teacher Talk							Pupil			Total
	1	2	3	4	5	6	7	8	9	10	
1											0
2				1	2			3		2	8
3				1	1					1	3
4				3				19	1	1	24
5				6	12	1		41		5	65
6		1		1	4					1	7
7											0
8		5	2	8	41	2		125	1	9	193
9		1	1	1	2						5
10		1		4	3	3		5	3	37	56
Total	0	8	3	24	65	7	0	193	5	56	361
%	0	2	1	7	18	2	0	53	1	16	

i/d = 1.57

Teacher 39 Time: 9:18 - 9:49

Category	Teacher Talk							Pupil			Total
	1	2	3	4	5	6	7	8	9	10	
1	2			6	2	4	2		2		18
2	1	2		7	1	5		8	8		32
3		3		13	7	2		2		1	28
4	1	1	1	17	9	2	2	70	2	5	110
5		2		19	27	9	3	25	12	4	101
6		1		8	3	22	4	12	18	2	70
7				4	1	5	5	6	2	1	24
8	7	14	24	28	35	6	4	36	11	2	167
9	7	9	3	4	13	14	4	1	5	1	61
10				4	3	1		7	1	5	21
Total	18	32	28	110	101	70	24	167	61	21	632
%	3	5	5	17	16	11	4	26	10	3	

i/d = 0.83

Teacher 10 Time 9:40 - 10:05

Category	Teacher Talk							Pupil			Total
	1	2	3	4	5	6	7	8	9	10	
1										1	1
2			2	1	1			1		1	6
3			1	4	1		1	1		2	10
4		2	1	8	3	5	1	34	1	23	78
5		1		9	29	6	1		3	12	61
6		1	1	6	5	29		1	6	22	71
7				3	1					1	5
8		1	4	21	8	4		8		2	48
9	1		2	5	4	8			1	7	28
10		1	2	26	4	16	3	4	15	128	199
Total	1	6	10	78	61	71	5	48	28	199	507
%	*	1	2	15	12	14	1	10	6	39	

* < 1%   i/d = 0.22

Teacher 45 Time: 9:13 - 9:41

Category	Teacher Talk							Pupil			Total
	1	2	3	4	5	6	7	8	9	10	
1				1				1		2	5
2		1		3		2	1	1	2	2	12
3						4		1	4	1	10
4			2	1	1	6	1	20	2	4	37
5						1	2	1		1	5
6	1		1	3	2	18	4	8	10	26	73
7	1					2	42	34		11	90
8		3	3	14	1	13	28	7	2	12	83
9	3	3	3	4		10	5	3	2	11	44
10		5	1	11		16	9	6	22	143	213
Total	5	12	10	37	5	73	90	83	44	213	572
%	1	2	2	6	1	13	16	14	8	37	

i/d = 0.17

Figure 29. Interaction matrices of four teachers in the same school system.

also indicates that most of the silent or confused periods which were not extended (10–10) were followed by more teacher questions (10–4), directions (10–6), or by pupils initiating their own talk (10–9). Thus, many of T–10's questions received no pupil responses, indicating either that the questions were in some way inappropriately presented, or that behavioral ground rules within the classroom were not being observed.

In the case of T–45, lack of pupil responses are in part explained by Category 7, which indicates that 16 per cent of the period was spent by the teacher in criticizing her class. Referring to T–45's matrix, it can be seen that almost half of her criticisms were extended in nature (7–7). The 7–8 cell indicates that almost half of the pupil responses (Category 8) followed, not questions from the teacher (4–8), but criticisms by her. The 8–7 and 7–8 cells suggest a cycle composed of teacher criticism, pupil responses, and more teacher criticism.

The 10–10 cells of both T–10 and T–45 reflect many extended periods of silence or confusion, which anecdotal records reveal to be mainly the latter. Respectively, 25 per cent of the total observation periods of each teacher consisted of this type of interaction.

Considerably less management-directed communication occurred between the aggressive teachers and their pupils. By far the bulk of T–32's pupil responses were extended in length (8–8). The most frequently occurring sequel to a pupil response fell in the 8–5 cell, indicating that the teacher gave more information. Shifting to the 5–8 cell, it can be seen that teacher information was followed consistently by pupil responses, thus establishing a cycle of short informational exchanges.

The sequels to pupil responses in T–39's class were varied and included every interaction category. Inspection of the cells in Row 8 reveals that the most frequently occurring sequels were teacher praise (8–2), teacher acceptance of idea (8–3), teacher question (8–4), and teacher information (8–5).

Giving directions (Category 6), teacher criticism (Category 7), and silence or confusion (Category 10) all occupy time which would otherwise be devoted to teaching. When column percentages for these three categories are compared among teachers, it can be seen that nonfunctional time for each of the aggressive teachers totalled 18 per cent, while for the passive teachers it was 54 per cent and 66 per cent, respectively.

The major differences between the teaching styles of the two aggressive teachers and the two passive teachers can be summarized by the i/d ratios, which accompany the interaction matrices in Figure 29. The i/d ratios of the aggressive teachers were 1.57, and 0.83. For the passive teachers they were 0.22 and 0.17. These differences indicate rather succinctly the extent to which control-type verbalisms predominated over supportive-type verbalisms in the two teachers who had responded passively to negative logistical situations. These differences also suggest that the aggressiveness with which system support was pursued was negatively related to the extent to which these four teachers were preoccupied with the overt control of their pupils' behavior.

T–30 was described earlier in this chapter as one who experienced many classroom organizational and management problems after returning to her school system. These problems were slowly resolved through the support of a dynamic school principal. Recordings of classroom interaction made during T–30's first and second post-training years reflect some of the progress that was made. Figure 30 presents her interaction matrices for these two years. Her i/d ratio went from 0.03 the first year to 0.33 the second year. Although the total percentage of nonfunctional time (Categories 6, 7, 10) does not change between observations, inspection of matrices immediately reveals a dramatic change in one of the nonfunctional categories. From 25 per cent of the first-year sample, teacher criticism (Column 7) has diminished to 5 per cent in the second-year sample. The first-year matrix shows that considerable teacher criticism was extended in nature (7–7) or followed either pupil responses (8–7) or, more markedly, pupil-initiated talk (9–7), or periods of silence or confusion (10–7). The second-year matrix shows heavy criticism only following silence and confusion (10–7). While the second matrix presents less time in pupil-initiated talk than the first (Column 9), very little of it was followed by teacher criticism (9–7).

While T–30 spent less than one per cent of the first-year observation period in giving praise or encouragement to her pupils (Column 2) she spent five per cent of the period doing this during the second-year [18].

Almost half of the second-year observation period was spent in silence or confusion (Column 10) as opposed to approximately one-fourth of the first year. Extended periods of silence or confusion

Category	Teacher 30 Time: 10:13-10:33										Total
	Teacher Talk							Pupil			
	1	2	3	4	5	6	7	8	9	10	
1											0
2		1							1		2
3								2	1		3
4				1	1			9	1		12
5				1	5	3	1		6	2	18
6				2	1	21	6	10	19	14	73
7					1	12	41	9	21	18	102
8				4	4	11	8	1	3	3	34
9			3	2	4	14	36	3	6	7	75
10		1		2	2	12	10	2	16	52	97
Total	0	2	3	12	18	73	102	34	75	97	416
%	0	*	1	3	4	18	25	8	18	23	

* <1%   i/d = 0.03

Category	Teacher 30 Time: 10:31-10:56										Total
	Teacher Talk							Pupil			
	1	2	3	4	5	6	7	8	9	10	
1											0
2			2		4			4	14		24
3			2	2	2			2	2		10
4					2		20		4		26
5			4	2	8			8	14		36
6		4		2	6	10	2	4	12	36	76
7					4				2	20	26
8			2	8	2	8	2			2	24
9		4	8	2	12	12	2		4	16	60
10		16		6	12	26	20		28	134	242
Total	0	24	10	26	36	76	26	24	60	242	524
%	0	5	2	5	7	15	5	5	11	46	

i/d = 0.33

Figure 30.   Interaction matrices for Teacher 30 in her first two post-training years.

were doubled (10–10). These additional steady-states were actually periods of mild confusion occurring as pupils settled down to new activities. In the first year they were invariably periods of violent turmoil. It is clear, however, from the 66 per cent of nonfunctional teaching time of each observation, that this teacher still had many organizational and management problems to solve.

LONGITUDINAL INFORMATION

An original assumption was that during the four-year follow-up phase of the project considerable longitudinal information would be compiled relative to the systems, the teachers, and the pupils.

If four groups of 12 teachers could be followed for four years, three years, two years, and one year, respectively, certain cross-sectional information and certain subjective impressions developed during on-site visits could be validated or rejected on the basis of information produced by changes over the period of time. Classes I and II should have been especially potent sources of longitudinal information.

As indicated by Table IX, of the 37 persons who taught brain-

TABLE IX
Maximum Number of Years Teachers Taught Brain-Injured
Children in the Same School

| Class | N | Number of Years in Same School | | | |
		1	2	3	4
I	10	2	3	2	3
II	7	2	3	2	
III	8	6	2		
IV	12	12			
TOTAL	37	22	8	4	3

injured children for at least one year during the follow-up phase of the project, only three from Class I taught brain-injured children in the same schools for four years—and one of these was the project demonstration teacher; only four teachers from Classes I and II taught brain-injured children in the same schools for three years; and only eight teachers from Classes I, II and III taught brain-injured children in the same schools for two years. Of this last group, three teachers, even though remaining assigned to the same schools for a second year, saw the membership of their classes change almost completely because of administrative decisions based on system-wide problems (e.g., transportation of pupils). These figures account for 15 of the 35 teachers who composed Classes I, II, and III. The members of Class IV were in their initial post-training year during the final project year.

By the fourth post-training year, the three teachers from Class I who were in their fourth year of teaching brain-injured children, in the same schools had seen their class memberships turn over almost completely. All but two of their original pupils had been phased back into other public school classes. The four teachers who were in their third year of teaching in the same schools had seen between half and two-thirds of their classes turn over. Five of the eight teachers who were in their second years in the same schools had each returned one or two children to regular classes.

Upon returning to their systems after completing their project training, these teachers had opened classes for groups of extremely disorganized children. These were children who had been excluded or were at the point of exclusion from public schools. Through working days, nights, and weekends these teachers had gradually made inroads on the problem of their pupils' disorganized behavior. Countless out-of-school hours were devoted to conceptualizing, designing, and constructing teaching materials to meet the needs of pupils unresponsive to initial approaches. Large amounts of in-school time were devoted to establishing pupil tolerances for, and skills in dealing effectively with their environment. Most of these teachers eventually discovered that they had been leading nun-like existences during their first post-training years, with almost every waking moment devoted in some way to the furtherance of their teaching goals.

Over a two-to-three year period pupils began responding to the teachers' energy investments, to the point where abilities to attend to and profit from learning tasks were in evidence, and to the point where they could relate to others positively enough to be considered for some form of regular-class reintegration.

During the latter portion of the site visits to second-year teachers, and during the site visits to third-year teachers a common statement from all was, "That first year was something I hope I never have to live through again." Alongside these statements, however, were almost palpable feelings of pride in the gains their pupils had made during and since those first years. Blocks of time in ever-increasing sizes had been devoted to instruction, where before so much had been used in behavior management. With preconditions of formal learning established, many pupils were developing academic skills preparatory to regular-class reintegration. Principals, supervisors, and parents were especially full of praise for the jobs most of these teachers had done.

In many respects the histories of these teachers' classes were similar in process to popular novels, where the protagonist is initially faced with a set of insurmountable problems that all attempts by others have failed to solve. Using intelligence, training, creativity, and hard work the problems are gradually reduced to the point where the story has a happy ending.

After the happy ending of a novel the book is closed and put on the shelf, perhaps to be read again in the future for enjoyment of its pleasures. The happy ending of a group of brain-injured children is followed—for the teacher—by a new group of brain-injured children. A cycle has been completed and a new one begun. For the three Class I teachers referred to in this section, and for two Class II teachers, the year that they had hoped they would never again have to "live through" was once more upon them.

Some of them frankly confessed that they were tired, both physically and mentally, and somewhat depressed at the thought of starting all over again. These statements were made during final-year site visits, well into the new school year. By that time, these teachers had actually been working with their new groups for several months. At the present writing (spring semester), the teachers report slow but consistent progress, and all signs point to the fact that they will continue to teach their present classes, although they are both likely to be drafted into supervisory positions soon.

The extent to which the experience and insights gained through working with their first groups of brain-injured children will offset this new-cycle reaction in the bulk of the teachers can only be speculated upon. Possibly the problem is being overstated here, in view of the observed high rate of teacher and pupil mobility which militates against many teachers completing cycles with their classes, or classes completing cycles with their teachers.

As mentioned earlier, the process of recording and analyzing classroom interaction was introduced to the project during the final two years of the follow-up phase. Information dealing with this process (in usable form) began appearing in the literature shortly before this period. Obviously, complete longitudinal interaction data for the four years were not obtained; and those which were must be interpreted with a degree of caution, as explained earlier. Data which were obtained, however, will be used as partial documentation of statements to be made about the teachers who taught for two or more years in the same schools.

Table X presents the small i/d interaction ratios of the teachers

TABLE X

SMALL i/d RATIOS OF TEACHERS WHO TAUGHT B–I CHILDREN IN THE SAME SCHOOLS FOR TWO OR MORE SUCCESSIVE YEARS

Teacher	Small i/d Ratio	
	1965–66	1966–67
T–10	0.22	0.43
T–39	0.83	1.19
T–30	0.03	0.33
T–41	0.58	0.98
T–43	0.10	0.17
T–12	0.22	0.44
T–31	1.14	0.68
T–42	0.58	1.15
T–26	0.63	1.17
T–45	*	0.17
T–22	0.60	†
T–18	0.54	†
T–48	0.26	0.63
T–21	**	†
T–33	**	†

* Recording not attempted; class too distractible.
** Recording not possible because of acoustical characteristics of room.
† No longer teaching a class of brain-injured children.

who taught the same classes of brain-injured children for two or more years (see Table IX). These ratios were computed from interaction records compiled during the final two years of the project. It will be noted that complete pairs of ratios are presented for only 10 of the 15 teachers. The classrooms of T–21 and T–33 did not lend themselves acoustically to the recording of verbal interaction. By the final year of the project T–21 and T–33 had both left this field of teaching. For the entire duration of the site visit performed in T–45's classroom in the 1965–66 school year, relations between the teacher and her pupils were so tense (see case study, p. 118) that project personnel deemed it inadvisable to attempt any recording, feeling that this would only add to the general tension level. By the following school year the situation had altered somewhat, and interaction recording yielded a small i/d ratio of 0.17. The matrix from which this ratio was computed appears in Figure 29. It shows that the teacher spent 30 per cent of the time making control statements (categories 6 and 7), as opposed to 5 per cent of the time in statements of a more supportive nature (categories 1, 2, and 3).

Of the 10 teachers upon whom complete pairs of i/d ratios are presented, in every case save one the 1966–67 ratios were markedly higher than the 1965–66 ratios. Increases ranged from 0.07 to 0.57, with a mean increase of 0.34 and a median increase of 0.36. The direction in which these changes occurred indicates that during the 1966–67 site visits the teachers made much less use of control statements and correspondingly more use of statements of affect or praise. The one teacher who reversed this trend had been working in the final phase of her first cycle of children during the 1965–66 visit, and by the time of the 1966–67 visit was working with a new group of children (plus two holdovers from her first group).

SUMMARY

During the four-year training phase of the project 48 grants were awarded to 47 experienced classroom teachers. Each of four classes spent a full academic year in a program designed to prepare them as teachers of brain-injured children.

The teachers were sent by twenty-eight public school systems and a Roman Catholic teaching order. The systems were furnished criteria for selecting the teachers to be sent. Upon entering into commitments to send the teachers' administrators to a one-week seminar in the spring of their training years, and to establish classes appropriate to the teachers' project training upon their return, the systems were allowed complete freedom in selecting the teachers to be sent. The single qualification to this was that each teacher must satisfy graduate school of education entrance requirements.

Twenty of the teachers were selected by the systems via a screening process based on general intrasystem solicitations of applicants. Seventeen were pre-selected by the systems with no general solicitation of applicants. Ten teachers initiated their own attendance by informing their systems of the project's existence; these systems subsequently entered into the stipulated commitments and sent the ten teachers.

The 47 teachers ranged in age (at the beginning of their training years) from 24 to 56 with a mean C.A. of 35 years, six months. The group was composed of 13 males and 34 females. Prior teaching experience ranged from 1 to 26 years, with a mean of 7.8 years. Forty-two had taught at the elementary level from 1 to 26 years. Eight had taught at the secondary level from 1 to 11 years. Of this last group, four had also taught at the elementary level. Twenty-five teachers held bachelor's degrees in education. An additional six held both bachelor's and master's degrees in education. Sixteen others had non-educational baccalaureate degrees, though five of them did have master's degrees in education.

As reflected by the *Minnesota Teacher Attitude Inventory,* the variation between the teachers in their abilities to develop effective interpersonal relationships with students rather closely resembled those of a norm group of elementary teachers. The MTAI raw score mean for the teachers was 54.5, whereas for the norm group it was 55.1. The project teachers' within-group percentile ranks were almost identical to those of the norm group. There were no significant between-class differences on this measure.

When the teachers were grouped by system selection modes, the mean MTAI score of the Pre-selected group was 17 points higher (non-significant) than that of the General Solicitation group. The mean MTAI score of the Self-Initiated group was 28 points higher than the Pre-selected group, a difference significant at the 0.01 level. The mean difference between the Self-initiated and Pre-selection group was non-significant.

The *Dogmatism Scale* revealed no significant differences in general authoritarianism between the teacher group and a group of graduate students in special education. As measured by this instrument, however, the teachers were significantly less authoritarian than a group of graduate students in vocational rehabilitation.

In the four initial post-training years of the four classes of teachers, 75 per cent were employed either as teachers of brain-injured children or as administrators of such programs. The remaining 25 per cent were almost equally divided between classes of emotionally disturbed children and non-special education positions. In the final project year, these over-all percentages had changed only slightly (to 77 per cent and 23 per cent), although many teachers' roles had changed in the intervening years.

Of 37 teachers who taught brain-injured children for at least one year during the follow-up phase of the project, three did so in the same schools for four years; four taught in the same schools for three years; eight taught in the same schools for two years. Of the last group, three saw their class memberships change almost completely during their second years because of administrative decisions not directly connected with the classes. These figures account for 15 of the 35 teachers who composed the first three training classes. The members of Class IV were in their initial post-training year during the final project year. All of Class IV were teaching brain-injured children at this time, though one had accepted a doctoral fellowship for the following year.

In the final two years of the follow-up phase of the project, the Flanders System of Classroom Interaction Analysis was introduced as a framework for describing social-emotional climates within classrooms.

Teacher-pupil interaction was recorded by project personnel during site visits to 30 of the 37 teachers who had taught brain-injured children. (Classroom acoustics ruled out most of the other 7.)

Ratios (i/d) were computed between the occurrences of indirect-supportive and direct-control statements of each teacher. (The i/d ratio increases in direct proportion to the extent to which indirect-supportive statements exceed direct-control statements.) On a cross-sectional basis, there were no significant differences between the i/d ratios of those in their first year of teaching brain-injured children and those who had been teaching brain-injured children for one or more years. On a longitudinal basis, within the set of teachers who had taught for two or more years, a trend appeared indicating that during the second year in which teacher-pupil interaction was recorded, less of the interaction was accounted for by control or managements statements.

REFERENCES

1. W. M. Cruickshank, Frances A. Bentzen, F. H. Ratzburg, and Mirian T. Tannhauser, *A Teaching Method for Brain-Injured and Hyperactive Children,* Syracuse University Special Education and Rehabilitation Monograph Series 6 (Syracuse, N.Y.: Syracuse University Press, 1961).

2. N. G. Haring and E. L. Phillips, *Educating Emotionally Disturbed Children* (New York: McGraw-Hill Book Company, Inc., 1962).

3. W. W. Cook, C. II. Leeds, and R. Callis, *Minnesota Teacher Attitude Inventory: Manual* (New York: The Psychological Corporation, n.d.).

4. N. A. Flanders, *Interaction Analysis in the Classroom* (Ann Arbor: University of Michigan, 1966), 4. (Mimeographed.)

5. One female was awarded a second grant to pursue doctoral-oriented study in the area of brain-injury, making a total of forty-eight awards.

6. Cook, Leeds, and Callis, *op. cit.,* 3.

7. M. Rokeach, *The Open and Closed Mind* (New York: Basic Books, Inc., 1960), p. 183.

8. *Ibid.,* 71–80.

9. N. A. Flanders, *Teacher Influence, Pupil Attitudes, and Achievement,* U. S. Department of Health, Education and Welfare, Office of Education, Cooperative Research Monograph No. 12, 1965.

10. *Ibid.*

11. Flanders, *Interaction Analysis in the Classroom,* 4.

12. Flanders, *Teacher Influence, Pupil Attitudes, and Achievement.*

13. E. Amidon and S. Simon, "Teacher-Pupil Interaction," *Review of Educational Research,* XXXV (1965), 130–39.

14. Rokeach, *op. cit.,* 182–95.

15. Flanders, *Teacher Influence, Pupil Attitudes, and Achievement,* 35.

16. *Ibid.*

17. *Ibid.,* 23–30.

18. None of the teachers had any knowledge of the nature of the information being recorded by project personnel in either of these years.

CHAPTER IV

Barriers to Innovation

The Training Program

Programs for the preparation of teachers and others who work with children in the public school systems must be closely attuned to the mechanics of introducing change in public education. The teacher preparation program alone is not the only agent for change; it is but one, albeit an important agent. Other factors which are equally as important, or in many cases more important than the teacher education program, include such things as the readiness of the community itself for innovation, the skills of administrators and others in interpreting the need for change into action programs, supporting legislation and financial programs, and other similarly significant and far-reaching factors. In this section, however, only the program of teacher preparation itself will be considered. Several important aspects of this problem need to be considered both in terms of the specific program involved and in terms of the broader issues of teacher education.

The nature of the teacher education program for hyperactive and brain-injured children which was utilized in this project has been outlined in some detail in Chapter II of this report. What is the relevance of this program to the demands which were made on teachers when they returned to their school communities? What was done during the program; what was needed or was not needed in terms of what was done?

TIME

It might be well to think first in terms of the duration of the training program itself. It will be recalled that two university

157

semesters were devoted to the preparation of the teachers. This proved insufficient. The assumption on the part of the university officials was that experienced teachers who knew children well would be able to adapt quickly to new ideas, to accept them as valid ideas to be tried, and to organize their energies in learning ways to implement these ideas effectively.

Four years of experience with four different groups of teachers demonstrated subjectively that this cannot be done in the short space of a nine-month university year, or that, if it can be done, the approach which was used was not the most effective way of insuring success. It is probably too much to expect that any teacher will be able to discard immediately much of what she has been taught and has found to be valid with normal children and to completely accept concepts which, on the surface, appear to be quite foreign to conventional educational practice. It is too much to expect that concepts which have been developing for two or three decades in the minds of university professors can be accepted with equal comprehensiveness by teachers when they come upon them for the first time. Experience in the teacher education program demonstrated that most of the first four or five months of the training year was spent by the individual teachers in trying to reorient themselves to the nature of the problem, to reconsider accustomed educational practices in the light of the different learning problems of brain-injured children, to assimilate fully a total concept of psychopathology on which the details of an educational rationale and method was intimately based, and to begin to think in an interdisciplinary rather than in a disciplinary frame of reference. While some of these elements have been recommended as sound in educational practice for many years, the extent to which teachers actually put them into practice, or the extent to which they are seen by teachers to be operational, is minimal. Yet in the program which was being suggested as the model, these were elements which were considered essential to the successful teaching of brain-injured and hyperactive children and which teachers would be expected to put into successful practice immediately. The extent to which intellectual and emotional acceptance of all of these concepts could be achieved by the teachers, in the face of what they knew to be the reality of their sending school systems, varied from teacher to teacher. On the whole, however, it is obvious that much more time than was permitted is required in order that orientation and reorientation be achieved.

From the above examples, one or two might be further considered. It was mentioned that teachers had difficulty in moving from accepted elementary educational practices to those which were recommended and which appeared to be contrary to good educational practice. In the education of normal children, the emphasis is customarily placed on the development of concepts which are closely related to one another. Reading, for example, will often follow along concepts which originated in the social studies. Spelling will grow out of reading. Art and music activities will relate as closely as possible to concepts, interest areas, or ideas inherent in the social studies or in reading materials. Integrated units having internal close relationships are stressed. With the hyperactive and brain-injured children, the opposite may be required. A child who is perseverating may have to be presented with activities which, instead of blending into one another, have diametrically opposite or different elements. Reading is followed, not by spelling or handwriting which utilize concepts from the reading activity, but by block design activities, motor training or parquetry work. Motor training may be followed by number concepts which are in turn superseded by peg board activities, and so on through the day. The reorientation of the teacher from one approach which she has found useful and successful with normal children to another approach which she has never tried, and for a population of children with whom she has never yet worked, is not a transition which can be made quickly or easily. Time for assimilation, opportunity for practicum experiences, opportunities for discussion, critique, and assessment, must be provided in greater number than is possible within the time limitations established in this project.

A second example of the problem faced by teachers and by university faculty is the following. In a typical elementary education program serving normal children, a reading lesson or an arithmetic lesson may occupy twenty to twenty-five minutes. The attention span of normal children usually permits them to function profitably for this period of time. The hyperactive or brain-injured child may be unable to attend to a given task for more than a minute or two, particularly in the initial stages of his new educational program. This means that instead of presenting the child with an arithmetic drill experience, for example, which might include a dozen two- or three-digit addition problems normally to be completed within twenty minutes at one sitting, the teacher may have to provide the child with ten or twelve one- or two-minute arithmetic lessons during the day, and thus permitting the child to operate at an optimum within his usable period of attention control. This is a different concept, and one with which teachers are generally unfamiliar. On the other hand, if the needs of the hyperactive and brain-injured child are to be met adequately, a program geared to his needs must be conceptualized. Time is required to assimilate, to accommodate, and to accept what at first must appear as a strange and unusual approach to educational practice by a teacher who comes to it with no background of similar experience with handicapped children.

Quantitative evidence for the need of additional time is lacking in this project. Qualitative evidence, however, was available to the faculty on numerous occasions. The spontaneous expressions of the teachers indicated their need for more time to assimilate ideas. Conflicts which developed between teachers, and between teachers and university faculty members were often the result of pressures felt by the teachers to accept without fully understanding, or having the time to understand the concepts completely. On the other hand, university faculty members, realizing the enormous amount of material yet to be covered, urged acceptance and practice while recognizing that the way was not fully prepared for complete understanding. The result was often tension and resistance. Opinions were expressed on many occasions by the most mature of the student group which indicated the great strain the teachers were under. Letters received by the university faculty after teachers returned to their school systems often reflected this need for time to think. "If only we could have thought to the point of complete acceptance or rejection, it would have been wonderful. As it was, because of the tremendous mass of material to be covered, experiences to be gained, projects to be completed for our future reference, we accepted without really knowing why we accepted," one thoughtful and skilled teacher wrote a few weeks after leaving the university. This student expressed an important criticism for the majority, if not for all of those who participated during each of the four years.

If the preparation program is as important as these authors consider it to be, it then follows that time sufficient to fully accomplish its goals must be provided. In the total field of special education, there is a growing recognition among university and public educational officials that short-term summer study is not the most satisfactory method by which to obtain skilled specialist teachers. At one time in the history of special education in the United States, this was practically the only procedure which could be used for special preparation. Rather, it is accepted that full-time study, logically planned, with rich libraries, varied study opportunities, and with time for contemplation, synthesization, and integration is essential. Similarly, with teachers of the hyperactive and brain-injured child, long-term study is apparently essential. Because of the complex nature of the educational problem and because of the unique differences both in the children and in the educational methods which are required to meet their needs, a longer amount of time than may be appropriate in other fields of special education appears warranted. Just what the optimal amount of time will be is not yet known. These authors feel strongly that more than two academic semesters is required. It is very likely that this phase of special education should be conceptualized in terms of a two-year masters degree program, or as a certificate of advanced study which normally includes the second year of graduate study. At the least, the program should be of twelve months' duration. However, the latter would depend upon the possibility of creating appropriate types of educational experiences for the teachers during the summer period. Until such time as universities and colleges move completely to a twelve-month educational program, the summer study experience appended onto a two-semester program is rarely more than just that—an appendix. These authors would prefer to visualize the program as one to cover the full two academic years, and to include informal camp or clinic experiences with hyperactive and brain-injured children during the intervening summer.

COURSEWORK

The nature of the formal courses which were included in the program, or which might be recommended for future programs, is naturally dependent in part on the factor of time which has just been discussed. There is little question in the minds of these writers but that university faculty members with broad experience and long specialization in the education of hyperactive and brain-injured children are necessary. This is not a program which can be taught by the dilettante. This is a full-time, career responsibility. However, it cannot be expected that all university faculty members who teach collateral courses will be specialists in the education of these children. In reading, for example, the university program should be able to include faculty members who are specialists in teaching reading to children with organic problems. The problems of the dyslexic child should be fully understood by the faculty members from that department both in the theoretical and in the clinical sense. The program should not include courses in speech simply because communication problems are important. It is essential that the organic problems basic to expressed speech be the emphasis in the speech pathology courses included in the program. As a matter of fact, one of the serious limitations of the present program was the absence of a full course in speech pathology and communication disorders of the brain-injured child. Some exposure to these problems was included in the program as has been indicated, but lack of time again limited this to what was an insufficient emphasis to provide complete understanding and competency. The need for a diversity of courses relating to the brain-injured child —in reading, speech pathology, neurology, sensory psychology, and motor training among others—immediately indicates that the program of teacher preparation in this aspect of special education is one which must be reserved to large universities with great resources upon which to draw. This is not a program for a small college with limited faculty resources.

In the present program, it will be recalled that a specialized seminar dealing with educational theory and methods with brain-injured and hyperactive children was included with a value of nine semester credit hours. This is certainly minimal. In an optimal program covering a two-year period, this seminar should logically be continued as a six semester-hour experience each semester for the entire length of the training period. Thus in two years, twenty-four semester hours would be assigned to this phase of the program which would include extensive examination of psychopathology, educational theory and historical background, educational methods, practices and teaching materials. It is felt that this amount of time is necessary in terms of the complexity of the problem and of the unusual nature of the children and their educational and life adjustment needs.

PRACTICE TEACHING

While relatively extensive direct contact was planned in the present program between teachers and hyperactive brain-injured children, it was insufficient. It was also limited essentially to one-to-one experiences of a tutorial nature. This type of experience has great values for the teacher as well as for the child, but it is not the pattern which the teacher will experience in the typical school system. A program of teacher preparation must be consistent, and must be of sufficient length so that the teacher-in-training can observe growth changes and can evaluate the impact on the children of her teaching activities and approach. Thus, it would be recommended that the tutorial experiences described earlier in Chapter II be continued, but that in a fully developed two-year program, one semester of the second year be devoted to practice teaching under supervision. This would include a full half-day, five days per week with a group of children. This immediately means that the site of the training program must be in a university which is in a community large enough to support several classes of brain-injured and hyperactive children which can be made available to practice teaching experiences. It is felt that the practice teaching experience is essential for all teachers, in spite of the fact that they may have had a number of years of successful teaching experience with normal children. Any teacher of normal children who has moved into this phase of special education is quick to attest to the fact that the two teaching experiences are extraordinarily different, and that little which was found valid in the one holds for the other.

If for no other reason than the mystique of brain injury, all teachers need experience with these children to provide them with the assurance required to operate independently at a later date.

TEAM LEADERSHIP

It has been stated that many teachers in the present program encountered difficulty in implementing their programs upon return to their school systems. In large part this was due to two reasons. First, they were unprepared for the leadership role which they were forced to assume, and they were unprepared to deal with the threat which this leadership role created for administrators or other professional colleagues when it was aggressively assumed. Second, while the concept of the team is not new in educational systems, its realistic and continued use is seldom encountered. Rarely also does the team include the classroom teacher in anything but a passive role if it is an active part of the pupil personnel program of a school system. In the present educational method, both the team and the participation of the classroom teacher as an active member of the team are vital elements.

While these problems and their concomitant issues were discussed with the project teachers, and while some observation of team function was provided for the teachers during the training period, this was insufficient to permit them to function smoothly in these areas upon their return to the school system. In an optimal program, courses in dynamics of human behavior, seminars dealing with power-structure concepts, the role of authority, and procedures for effective change should be included in the training period. Each teacher should be given the opportunity to participate actively in the interdisciplinary team during the period of her practice teaching and to observe frequently the operation of smoothly functioning teams of professional people.

The role of motor training in the education of brain-injured children is not one on which there is complete professional agreement. However, it is the opinion of these authors that it plays a unique and significant role in the total educational program when it is appropriately integrated with other elements equally essential. However, motor training for children, as an inherent aspect of the educational program, is not something with which elementary teachers are fully conversant. In the present program, beginning with Class II, a significant amount of time was devoted to an understanding of and methods of carrying out a motor-training program with brain-injured hyperactive children. It is the feeling of the authors, following the post-training evaluation visits, that the amount of time allocated to this was generally insufficient. At least the equivalent of six semester credit hours of training involving both theory and practice should be provided over the first year of the optimal program.

These authors also feel that a significant amount of *additional course experience* in such matters as educational assessment techniques, interpretation of test data, mental hygiene, psychology of learning, and parent education is essential. From an examination of the course program outlined in Chapter II, it will be seen that these aspects were included in other courses or seminars, but not as major parts. The optimal program will carry each of these as a major emphasis in its own right. It should not be assumed that the authors are seeking a lengthy and complex program just for the sake of filling in a time block. To the contrary, it is their feeling that no phase of special education can tolerate mediocrity, and especially is this true in the complex issues of hyperactivity and brain-injury. Teachers of quality are needed for what is probably the most complex of all special educational problems. The elements which are being suggested here are those which in part will lead to the high quality in educational programs parents and thoughtful educators expect the schools to provide, and which hyperactive and brain-injured children must have in order to make a satisfactory adjustment in society.

RESIDENT COORDINATOR

The writers do not wish to belabor the issue of complexity, but the fact of the matter is that the education of these children is uniquely complex. We have stated that teachers require time to assimilate new ideas and to make important educational adjustments to a different teaching approach, but time alone is not sufficient to insure the desired outcome. Teachers seeking to prepare themselves to serve these children need much opportunity to talk with others, to rationalize concerns, to obtain assurance that they really are on the right path, to experiment, to be discouraged and to experiment again. During the four years of the program at Syracuse University the project director spent a considerable amount of his time in a type of individual counseling relationship with the teachers which provided for some of these needs. Another faculty member spent at least a fourth of the available time in a similar capacity, but more time for individual student-teacher contacts was obviously needed. The writers feel that every university teacher education program of this type should set aside at least a portion of one faculty member's time, so that he can function as a resident coordinator and as a continuing counselor to teachers-in-training. The extent to which this type of service can be provided to teachers will influence the degree to which secure teachers are returned to their school systems prepared to enter into an exacting educational experience.

It is indeed time that colleges and universities recognize that the preparation of quality teachers also involves a considerable degree of psychotherapeutic emphasis as well. Teachers approach children with all of the historical stereotypes and misconceptions of the society from which they come. They approach children in terms of their own biases and religious concepts, as well as in terms of their long-standing moral and ethical ideas. Clashes between teacher and child are often the result of the failure to blend two cultures; the failure of the teacher to empathize fully with the cultural background and orientation of the child, or the guilt which the teacher may feel in her inability either to accept the language or behavior of the children or her inability to modify quickly the child's personal behavior and adjustment. Many of these potential problem areas will become evident to university faculty members during the teacher preparation period, both during formal class and seminar experiences and during clinical and practice teaching programs. When tensions develop within a teacher, there must be someone with whom she can relate in order to deal with them on a valid psychotherapeutic basis. The resident coordinator may well be the individual who can fill this role most adequately. He must not only be one who understands the nature of the teacher education program in its theoretical and practical implications, but must also be one who can relate fully to the teachers who are participating in the program.

One of the roles which a resident coordinator can effectively accomplish is to help to provide teachers with a good orientation to the problems which they will face upon return to their school systems. There should be an opportunity for teachers to express their concerns as well as their hopes for accomplishment. Teachers need assistance in techniques for dealing with administrative stumbling blocks and inertia. They need a thorough understanding of the appropriate professional roles which they will play on the interdisciplinary team. They need support in the knowledge that they may not be accepted as members on the interdisciplinary team by persons of other professions who may never before have worked with educators in a dynamic relationship. These are not concepts which can be given to teachers in a general lecture; they are concepts which must be discussed in small groups or individually, in such a way that complete understanding and personalized meanings are obtained. The psychotherapeutic role of the resident coordinator is a significant one in this regard.

DEVELOPMENT OF SELLING SKILLS

At this stage in the historical development of special education programs for hyperactive and brain-injured children, there is a need for a type of teacher preparation which, hopefully, is transitional. Generalizations here may be misinterpreted, yet it is the considered opinion of these authors that generalizations are possible and accurate. Special education has always had to be aggressive in its own right, since, as a concept, general elementary educators and administrators have rarely taken the initiative to accept it. There is much evidence for these statements, both legal as well as practical.

If educators were indeed completely sincere in their stated goals of meeting the needs of all children in American schools, special legislation for the protection of disabled children would not be needed. Yet such legislation is to be found in every state. Special education is permissive in some, mandated in others. Legislation *per se,* however, has been found necessary in order to provide even the basic educational services to disabled children.

This situation is not entirely a reflection of apathy or hostility of educators alone toward the disabled child. It is a reflection of the historical and social attitudes of which education and disability are but important elements. The total social order—the community as a whole—often reflects guilt feelings regarding disabled persons, including children. These are often reflected in neglect, in hostility gilded over by veneers of emotion and sympathy, by needs to publicly display concern and acceptance, or by avoidance of situations which remind one of the presence of disability. These are not figments of the imagination! They are demonstrable elements in the everyday life of society. Parents of handicapped children constantly must fight, individually and collectively, for every service which is needed by their children.

The frequent reluctance of the community to face the needs of the disabled person except after prolonged prodding is obviously reflected in the programs of the public schools. It is certainly reflected in the individual attitudes of school board members, superintendents, principals, guidance and psychological personnel, and teachers. There are many exceptions to these statements, but the fact of the matter is that they represent the truth in all too many instances. These attitudes are reflected in the ease with which school administrators move special classes for the disabled from room to room, building to building. They are reflected in the location of special classes within a given building, a matter so serious in some communities that states have had to provide special regulatory measures to keep these classes out of basements, away from boiler rooms, or from completely inadequate facilities outside of the school building itself. They are reflected in the lack of equipment and teaching materials so often observed, in the demands made upon the special teacher, in the lack of supportive services which should be provided, in what sometimes is noted to be active aggression on the part of some administrators and elementary and secondary teachers toward the special education program. These factors are related to teacher preparation. In this particular program of teacher preparation there are documented observations made many, many times duing the post-training evaluation period. These attitudes are not new or specific to this field of special education; they have been dynamic and observed throughout the history of education in America. They are religiously, politically, historically, and psychologically oriented and founded. They are attitudes which, at this writing, are almost as dynamic and active as they were a hundred years ago when the foundations for special educations were being laid down in the United States.

If special education is to succeed, teachers of the disabled child must be taught how to be agents of action. They must be given the techniques for promoting change to which the change target may be resistant. Teachers of hyperactive and brain-injured children, in particular, must be given techniques and understandings in these matters, for the very nature of the education program for these children runs counter to so much of what is traditional in general elementary education. Class size, one-to-one teaching, use of assistants, structure, interdisciplinary concepts, length of teacher preparation, disuse of the traditional report card—all these, and many other aspects of the educational program constitute exceptions to the general rules of the school. These exceptions, compounded by deep-seated notions regarding disability in general, constitute tremendous hurdles for teachers to overcome. Without much thought and insight into the nature of attitudes which will be expressed, into the dynamics of program development, into the nature of interdisciplinary programming, or into the subtle reasons for obvious inertia the teacher becomes introspective and feels guilty that she has failed in her mission. Colleges and universities have not given sufficient thought to the preparation of the teacher as an agent for change. This is a role which special education teacher education programs must assume if the needs of all children in American schools are to be met.

It was initially stated that this aspect of the teacher education program might well be transitional in nature. The attitudinal situation here being discussed does change. It has changed to a more positive level in the past fifty years and it continues to change for the better. Many school principals and general school administrators make genuine plans for disabled children within their schools. Many accept these children and the implications of their needs for educational programs fully and honestly. The attitudes expressed by many people during the evaluation phase of this project, however, indicate that healthy attitudes of acceptance are not universal. Teachers of hyperactive and brain-injured children must be prepared to face and to cope with negative attitudes and hostility without developing introspective guilt feelings. Teachers of special education often *care too much,* an attitude which may be the result of hostility faced daily. Until such time as society and its representatives fully accept all children as equals and are willing, without compulsion, to provide for the needs and growth of *all* children, teachers of special education must be given the assistance which is needed to cope with anything less than optimal conditions. This is a large responsibility of the teacher education center—the college or the university. In another program of teacher education with hyperactive and brain-injured children this is a facet of the training which would be greatly emphasized by these authors.

TEACHER SELECTION

There were suggestions in certain parts of the data that the teachers who initiated their own applications to the training project manifested more positive attitudes toward educating children than did those who were selected by systems. A nonsignificant statistical trend appeared which indicated that the pre-selected teachers were characterized by more positive attitudes than were those teachers from systems in which general solicitations had been made prior to screening and selection. Within all the selection-mode groups, however, there were wide variations, both in test scores and in post-training performance, indicating that the modes of teacher selection employed by the sending systems did not operate to any extreme degrees of internal consistency. An example of this is the performance of the selection committee mentioned in the preceding chapter. In the years of its operation the composition of the committee changed several times, and applicants who had been turned down as unqualified in previous years were subsequently among those selected and sent to the project.

These findings, plus the more general observation that in terms of the characteristics observed these teachers were not different from any average or randomly selected group of teachers, argued against an assumption which project personnel had held as implicit in system functioning. This was that the systems could and would consistently select uniquely capable personnel for a specialized training program, once they had been informed of the characteristics to be looked for in the candidates.

Some of the teachers who most clearly satisfied selection criteria were sent as the result of intensive evaluation. Many others in this group were apparently sent by chance. The same held true for any dimension in which the teachers' characteristics were grouped.

Considered as a group of systems, the abilities of some to select outstanding teachers was unfortunately counterbalanced by others which deliberately sent teachers so as to avoid or postpone the resolution of local personnel problems. One system unabashedly admitted having done this. A few others were less frank about their motives, but the post-training program assignments of their teachers left few questions in the minds of project personnel.

It became apparent that the teacher selection criteria had been presented to the sending systems in a form incapable of objective measurement by them. Only subjective information was available, for instance, to support the systems' decisions that a teacher was "skilled in a one-to-one teaching situation," was "acceptant of slow progress in children," or was "able to establish warm relationships between self and children." If these were qualities deemed necessary, then the systems should have been provided with objective means for identifying and measuring them or with a more specific set of characteristics. This should have been one part of a comprehensive pre-project communication effort on the part of project personnel.

Some local decision-making figures operated selection machinery while having only the vaguest notions as to the nature of the training program to which the teachers were being sent. Project personnel had evidently done an inadequate job of communicating the specific purposes of the program at the times when system involvements were initially obtained. While explanations in detail were made to high-level personnel at those times, necessary steps were not always taken to relay this information to personnel at lower levels—including the prospective teachers themselves.

This lack of information was invariably manifested later; at the administrators' seminar, and when the teachers returned to their systems. The misconceptions and unpreparedness of some systems at those times proved to be major negative factors in the quest for professional and logistical program support.

Obviously, graduate school entrance requirements should not have constituted the limits of project involvement in the selection process. It is difficult to stipulate even at this point, however, what the extent of project involvement should have been. Project personnel should have become extremely knowledgeable about both the teachers and their systems prior to making selection decisions. This would have necessitated their presence in each system for indefinite periods of time. This was obviously not feasible, considering the number of school systems involved and their widespread geographic disposition. This is not to be construed as questioning the logic of that type of involvement, however. Very obviously, if teachers are to be sought who meet specific qualitative criteria, and if the subsequent support and cooperation of their school systems is to be obtained, then there must be very close and effective contact and communication between the universities and the schools.

For purposes of this discussion, the logic of this type of involvement could only be questioned upon remembering that guidelines were being sought for the establishment of training programs for large numbers of teachers at many different universities. At this level of discussion, it can only be said that a training model was being examined; a selection-training model was needed.

The process of bringing candidates to the campus for assessment was not used because it was felt that optimal selection decisions *could* be made by the systems, and in order to elicit from them certain investments which would operate toward providing the necessary system supports for the teachers upon the completion of their training.

Since the training group that was assembled did not appear to differ greatly from what any group might have resembled if chosen randomly from the universe of elementary school teachers, additional project attention to the selection function might have, at the very least, had a positive effect on the lower end of the distribution.

The question may be raised as to the extent to which graduate level teacher preparation programs can reasonably expect to enroll positively atypical teachers in their programs in large numbers year after year. It is certainly assumed that these large numbers exist, but the competition for their time by the public schools, the universities, and by other educational agencies, may obviate against their inclusion in consistently large numbers. Perhaps more significantly, they do not seem to be as easily identified by their own administrators as might have been assumed.

Until now any but the most conventional of graduate level teacher preparation programs have operated mainly on pilot bases, with one-time selection efforts. The extent to which permanent programs resulting from these pilot ventures may be able to keep their classes filled with the types of individuals they most desire is certainly open to speculation. Following this line of thought, so is the extent to which graduate programs may be able to go in preparing less outstanding individuals for sophisticated educational functioning.

These authors do not feel for one moment that untalented individuals can or should be produced to work in what Schaefer has described as educational dispensaries.

. . . apothecary shops charged [only] with the distribution of information and skills deemed beneficial to the social, vocational, and intellectual health of the immature [1].

At the present time, however, it is probable that the long-range need for large numbers of educational specialists may have to be satisfied in some measure from parts of the general teacher population, in addition to the upper extreme of the distribution.

After Training, Then What?

The follow-up of a teacher training program is probably best understood in an evaluational sense where the effort is directed toward the determination of value. Concepts such as effectiveness, efficiency, logistics or strategy and even "ripples" are utilized in dealing with questions of evaluation. The determination of value is fixed upon or derived from a set of prior values.

The design problems that emerge when one tries to move from this essentially axiologic set into an experimental or research set has already been described, at least in relation to the present project.

Another way of understanding the follow-up of a teacher training program is in relation to the issues that emerge and can be understood as relevant to the training task. Listening to the problems of day-to-day operations of special programs and becoming empathic with the feelings of people about a different approach to educational methodology is a maturing experience. Some of these issues can be described. The authors cannot rely on any kind of "hard data" in doing this but can feel comfortable in sharing their perceptions based on hundreds of hours of listening. Since the authors' bias is that the field issues should become, in one way or another, training issues, it seems appropriate to share them in this context.

The education of brain-injured children cannot be adequately understood solely as an intramural issue, where major concerns are limited to the classroom. First of all, we are dealing with behavioral and performance deviation and, in this sense, have to extend our perception to include the meaning of any responses to behavioral deviation in a social as well as professional context. Second, we are dealing with children, who while not new to educators, bear labels (brain-injured) which tend to make them strangers to the education enterprise. Third, we are talking about children whose learning problems are extremely complex and require major cooperative effort among several disciplines to adequately understand each child. Fourth, we are viewing the issues in relation to one particular strategy of education that has been proposed as appropriate for these children. Fifth, we are dealing with a psychoeducational problem which makes at least as many, if not more demands on the teacher than any other problem to be dealt with in the public school. Sixth, the administrations, philosophies, technical orientation, and dynamics of school systems bearing basically upon all of the other issues take different forms in different systems.

In short, the issues and questions relevant to the education of brain-injured children spiral into multiple social and professional issues. The feelings and views of professional as well as lay groups, the organization of systems, the nature of interactions and, most generally, the dynamics of all processes geared to the development and implementation of quality education for children become relevant. The following is a discussion of some of these issues.

SYSTEM DYNAMICS

Ideally, systems are organized with decision-making functions at every level of the corporate body. An individual placed at a given system level is delegated responsibility and authority. His decisions are made within these responsibility-authority parameters. He is a professionally competent and creative person, and exercises sufficient initiative so that he maintains steady pressures against his responsibility-authority limits. He is involved in decisions made at levels both subordinate and superior to his own. He freely accepts the views of others, he values them and frequently incorporates them, but never allows them to serve as excuses for avoiding his own responsibilities. He makes his own views available to others without feeling unduly threatened by the myriad ways in which these views might be received or interpreted. He is constantly aware of his own intrasystem *raison d'être,* and focuses all of his abilities on goal-directed activities appropriate to his professional mission.

The organizational plans which specify intrasystem personnel relationships are official descriptions of each system's decision-making machinery. They identify positions at each level of decision-making and present these positions in flow-chart form so that the machinery can be followed from the highest to the lowest levels and vice versa.

Formal statements and schematics of the above nature were found to exist in most of the school systems which cooperated with the project. In a few others they only existed informally, on a commonly-agreed-upon basis. In some of the latter systems certain parts of organizational substructures had to be inferred by project personnel, as little had ever been done toward articulating them. Regardless of their modes of expression, however, these were all official system statements.

It frequently happens that these official statements are paralleled in part by unofficial, *de facto,* relationships which have considerable influence on system decisions. These *de facto* relationships are composed of varying combinations of the same sets of system ingredients which form the official statements. They can be either vertical or lateral in their modifying effects on the organizational structures.

De facto relationships are established in a variety of ways. They may be aggressively pursued by individuals who wish to by-pass others, either in getting decisions made or in seeing them implemented once they are made. They may be brought about through certain critical acts of omission: those which occur as a result of passive-aggressive attempts to influence events by inaction; and those which are caused by anxiety-ridden officials fearful of taking (what they perceive to be) risks. The end results of either type of modification-by-omission are usually the same as those of the aggressively pursued modifications. Targeted officials are frustrated but oblivious to what is ·happening, or they are frustrated and sensitized to the danger of their diminishing influence. Their reactions can be either passive (followed by loss of power) or aggressive. Aggressive reactions are directed to obtaining role clarifications, and pinpointing responsibilities. These may be accompanied by more covert attempts to build support for their positions (anyone can play the modification game).

From the standpoint of the observer, values may be attached to any observed modifications in terms of the efficacy of the official machinery in serving as a decision-making model, and in terms of the competencies of the individual officials found within that model. If both of these factors have highly positive valences, and are serving the legitimate needs of the system, then unofficial attempts to tamper with their relationships must be viewed somewhat negatively. If, on the other hand, the needs of the system are not being served, and if official modification attempts have been unsuccessful, then the observer may be inclined to view the situation less negatively, for, in many of these cases, those who would modify relationships within the model could only be accused of trying to make it work.

All of the school systems which sent teachers to the project were structured around viable administrative models. Many contained effective personnel at all levels. When this was the case innovation, subject to careful and continual scrutiny, was not feared. Personnel displayed enthusiasm and ingenuity in incorporating the concept of educational services to brain-injured children into their over-all service program. Honest differences in orientation and opinion regarding brain-injured children frequently existed, but these were bases of system strength which operated toward free and open exchanges of ideas.

Other systems were less fortunate in this respect. They each contained one or more individuals at different levels of responsibility who gave less than their full support to programs that had been approved at the very highest levels of their systems.

There were two basic reasons for this absence of support. One was a system variable wherein lines of authority and responsibility were unclear, and where the responsibilities of personnel with titles such as "coordinator," "supervisor," and "director" were not always matched with commensurate degrees of authority. Closely related to this was the other variable; personality.

A few key individuals in each of these systems had succeeded in unofficially modifying intrasystem decision-making and decision-implementation processes. This had been done aggressively, passive-aggressively, passively, and in varying combinations of these modes.

As an illustration of how these modifications are accomplished *aggressively* the following example is presented. Two pupil personnel workers, selecting and ignoring their cases with great care, continually presented "evidence" in support of their views and in negation of the views of other professionals in the same system. This was done for the benefit of school principals and for upper-echelon administrators. They were successful to the point where at times they wielded more actual influence over the program for brain-injured children than did the director of special education. This happened in a small city considerably removed from the nearest university. It appeared to project observers that these two individuals had a local monopoly on clinical and pseudo-clinical jargon, with few serious contenders present. One of these contenders was the newly appointed director of special education who is, as of this writing, spending a great deal of his energy in seeking his own modifications in the system's decision-making machinery.

A *passive-aggressive* example comes from a system where a

middle-echelon administrator with clearly defined responsibilities consistently reported not having received classroom equipment and supply requisitions at the times most critical for their inclusion in annual budgets. These requisitions always seemed to have been either mislaid or delayed in system channels on the way to his desk, or else they were made out improperly by teachers and principals, making it necessary for them to be returned. The fact that this administrator had a clear-cut responsibility for these types of paper-work transactions suggested to project observers that hidden motives were operating here. The loud complaints of the teachers about the additional long hours they were forced to expend in attempting to compensate for logistical deficiencies were used by this administrator as proof of the inefficacy of the project's strategy for educating brain-injured children.

A system in which the authority-responsibility parameters of certain middle-echelon administrative positions lacked clarity proved to be a fertile breeding ground for *passively* based modifications in system decision-making. A program supervisor was extremely reluctant to make decisions on issues pertaining to the classes of brain-injured children in the system's special education program. This passivity provided a vacuum into which other system personnel—including the teachers—moved whenever they developed strong feelings about any of the issues surrounding the classes. Pupil service personnel published pupil selection criteria that were sufficiently ambiguous to allow the inclusion of many children who could not be most adequately served by the educational model the teachers were prepared to implement. Psychologists gave these criteria liberal interpretations and filled at least one class almost completely with aggressive, socially disadvantaged, functionally retarded children. A social worker took upon himself the task of interpreting the aims of the program to parents of the pupils, without a clear understanding of what those aims actually were. One of the teachers established her own rather negative policies regarding the relationships between herself and other professionals in the system. As a result of this fragmented vacuum-filling, the program for brain-injured children had fallen into disrepute well before the end of its first year of operation. The original decision—made at the highest system level—to establish an educational program for these children failed in its implementation largely because of the passive acts of omission of an insecure middle-echelon administrator.

The *unofficial modification* of system decision-making machinery can sometimes have positive effects. This happened in several systems where programs for brain-injured children were inaugurated, through the aggressive efforts of various combinations of teachers, supervisors, principals, psychologists, directors, and assistant superintendents.

The influence that T–12 had on her system was described in an earlier chapter. This teacher had overtly solicited not only a major system decision, but had succeeded in obtaining enough personnel role modifications so that she was able to interact with other professionals with peer status during and after the pupil selection process.

T–17 and her principal aggressively effected enough modifications in their system's decision-making machinery to establish a program for brain-injured children by the beginning of T–17's second post-training year.

The director of special education mentioned in the aggressive example was working closely with his teachers in order to deal with the problems created by the pupil service workers. The situation here was similar to one which Redl has called the "resurrection of agency guilt." Redl was talking about community mental health agencies, but his interaction model can be applied here. After a long-needed service is finally developed within a system, the first pupils it receives are "punitive referrals."

. . . "punitive referrals" . . . by which I mean the agency refers kids it hopes that at least somebody else will fail with too. Besides, the new agency usually has to face the accusation of undue luxury and snobbism because it seems fancier, makes claims the original agencies did not make, and is usually temporarily highlighted a little beyond what jealousy-coping capacities can tolerate [2].

At this writing, the director is attempting to get the officially approved decision-making machinery restored to working order so that some degree of control can be obtained by him over matters dealing with pupil selection and program implementation. This director knows that his ends will not be realized by administrative fiats from on high, as these already exist in the form of the officially approved (but unofficially modified) machinery. He is working extremely closely with his teachers, aiming at maximal early success with the pupils in their classes. He is also using the teachers as resource persons and as speakers to other groups within the system. He knows that his chances of changing the biases of the two powerful pupil personnel workers are only slight, but hopes to convince the school principals in the system of the value of the program for brain-injured children, and in that way re-establish effective communication between their offices and his own.

A decision was made in another system to open classes for brain-injured children in a large elementary school, which happened to be the only one in the system with available space. The school principal was unalterably opposed to this. He was one of the system's veteran principals, and was totally unconvinced of the potential efficacy of any treatment save exclusion for behaviorally deviant children. An upper-echelon administrator was also a veteran within the system with equally long service. He had been instrumental in obtaining the original system-decisions to send teachers to the training project and to establish classes upon their return. Through the sheer exercise of his power within the system he placed the classes in that school, totally divorced from any contact with its principal, staff, or regular class children. The classes have their own private entrances, their own daily time schedules, separate systems of supply, and their own private telephone line. They report directly to him. At this writing the program has shown progress within the limits of this administrative stand-off. What will happen when pupil reintegration becomes imminent is open to considerable speculation.

Without presenting any further examples of decision machinery modifications, positive or negative, it can be safely stated at this point that in too many school systems too many people spend too much of their time planning and executing campaigns of interoffice combat. It would be easy (as the authors may have done here) to accept these conflicts in terms of the necessity for the "good guys" to fight the "bad guys," but these value assignments can be relative, depending upon the underlying motivation of the conflict behavior.

INVESTMENT: A NECESSITY AND A HAZARD

The work of teachers of brain-injured children has been described in several places in the literature. The intraclassroom demands on teachers have been viewed with appreciation for the physical and psychological demands that ensue from work with these children. These descriptions, however, have been predicated mostly on observations of classes in institutions or university demonstration classes, and classes in a very few public schools.

One unique perception to share as a result of following up the development of classes in school systems across the country has to do with extra classroom demands on and professional relationships of the project-trained teachers. They were to some extent the bearers of a body of information, a point of view that was frequently at variance with typically held conceptions. In part then, the local validation of these concepts, the burden of proof, fell upon the professional shoulders of the teachers. Their efforts and the responses to such efforts were extremely variable.

Conscientious teachers who face children daily, agonize at the failure of these children. They often regress to hoping for rapid major gains that they really know will be several months or a year or more in coming. Teachers are no more immune to rescue fantasies than other professionals. Realistic expectations for small increments of gain and occasional regression are often lost in the teacher's enthusiasm about a new idea. It is very easy for a teacher, hoping so much to teach a child, to be deluded by her own excitement over a new set of methods or materials. To see the ideas have little effect, or to have the materials received by Johnny with detachment or even the same destructive glee with which he accepted the toy that accidentally fell from Larry's pocket, has a human effect directly proportional to the investment of the teacher's self in the program.

These teachers, to whom Rappaport refers as "ego banks" for ego-bankrupt children, *have to care*. Sometimes they care too much. They risk hurt each time they allow involvement—yet involvement is essential. A classroom for these children is no place for a weak teacher (emotionally or physically). If her own psychological house is not in reasonable order, it will quickly become a shambles. Overworked defenses are not only emotionally exhausting to the teacher, but they spell almost certain failure for her efforts. A child who, in trying to be understood, has found himself psychologically mute, who finds himself in a perceptually disordered world where even his own physiognomy may not be a clear or complete picture, whose constant failure has precluded any feeling of self-worth, whose anger is so great that it frightens him as much as it does those toward whom it may be directed, is not likely to use to much advantage a program in which the teacher personalizes his behavior, denies her own feelings, displaces her own anger, or projects inappropriate interpretation on the child's behavior. In these instances an intolerable (for children and teacher) situation exists where ignorant armies do indeed clash by night.

The matter of investment is a serious one, often underestimated or misunderstood—especially by administrators. A teacher, as we have stated, must make great investments in her program if she is to be effective. Hers is not an eight-hour-a-day routine do-it-by-the-book job. In relating to administrators and supporting personnel, her investment, as well as the issues she is raising, must be heard (listened to and valued). Not to appreciate this dimension of the interaction often results in talking at cross-purposes and invites the loss of effective communication. The misalignment of investment is not infrequently the result of one side having only mediocre interest in and concern for the problem. This is an extremely difficult situation, and it forces the teacher to seek support from others who care and are willing to make some investment in hearing.

INNOVATION AND MAGIC

It has been the experience of the authors and others that when needs are identified in education and programs are proposed to meet them, the programs are not always accepted or rejected solely in terms of the efficacy of the model and its existent or nonexistent supporting data. Three factors worth mentioning here affect the over-all soundness of the program and may even determine the program's fate. These are: salesmanship skills of the program advocates, clarity of the model, and relative ease of administration. The incorporation of a new or different set of ideas is often predicated on some combination of these three variables. While these are real issues to be faced in an innovative process, they may militate against an experimental set in programming which is an essential aspect of any proposed educational strategy today.

The "salesmanship" issue, mentioned earlier in relation to the training program, is basically a matter of how dynamic the salesman is, how persuasive he can be, and his awareness of the political-professional channels where the introduction of his thinking will have the greatest impact. Ideas then get associated with that person to the extent that acceptance or rejection of a program becomes the acceptance or rejection of that person's thinking. This is unfortunate in a day when we need thinkers, innovators and evaluators, not disciples.

There is a subtle, yet very real difference between selling a program and interpreting or explaining it. The former is more akin to the process of indoctrination, the latter to professional education.

The authors wondered in some instances whether certain systems had been "sold on" the program model rather than having developed an evaluative belief in it. Using the distinction drawn here, the latter implies that reasonable changes can be made based on a rational frame of reference. The former implies that the program was implemented because it existed and happened to be the one to which the system was exposed.

It will become clear that the three variables (salesmanship, clarity, and relative ease of administration) are basically related. By clarity is meant the obviousness of the model form. Whether one is talking about carpets and cubicles or M&M's, these are parts of model forms. They are not educational ideas. They are instrumental artifacts of basic theoretical conceptions of learning and education. They are usable logical derivatives of a rationale. Apart from the rationale, the artifact or derivative makes little if any sense and cannot be used intelligently. Unless she has a frame of reference for determining when its use is or is not appropriate and how its use can be most effective, the teacher is herself used by such forms. It is little wonder that the forms and artifacts of educational rationales are sometimes attacked with animosity and discarded as inappropriate. Defeat in the eclectic exploitation of such forms is almost inevitable. The irrational, perhaps unconscious hope that few would admit to is that such forms hold some kind of endemic magic. The hope in some quarters of the behavioral and social sciences that magical answers and easy solutions will eventually emerge is not headline news. At one level the hope is an honest one and is symptomatic of the overwhelming nature of daily profession problems. Most typically, such hopes are held out by front-line staff who must cope with the realities of service. In education particularly, teachers, administrators, and supervisors are probably the most vulnerable to such hope.

Most frequently, those most hopeful for magical solutions are those most easily swayed by dedicated salesmen.

A footnote should be appended to this discussion. We are still in a crude state of the art of educating exceptional children. Our technical capability is lagging significantly behind social change. Commitment to the reasonable solution of basic human problems is far in advance of reliable and valid innovative responses to that readiness. This is not inconsistent with what has already been stated in that there is a fundamental difference in readiness to accept innovation, and willingness to approach innovation with an evaluative set based on reason and logic.

There has not yet been formed an adequate substitute for intellectual effort in appropriating even tentative answers. We cannot reason together, however, until we obtain a personal investment in reasonable solutions which rates candor and openness to differences as high in priority values. In a paper jungle where memoranda are the ties that bind and precedent too often the major defense against proposed action, such opportunity is rare.

The issues of clarity and readily familiar artifacts were particularly pertinent to the educational model to which the teachers were exposed. Cubicles, carpets, incandescent lighting, solid pastel-colored walls, absence of pictures, bulletin boards, pencil sharpener, and so forth are associated with the model. They are, indeed, considered logically consistent with the rationale which conceptualizes psychopathology primarily from the point of view of stimulus adjustment. They are, however, only logically consistent features when they are based on the particular learning characteristics of certain children at certain times. That is, all eight children in a class would not necessarily need to have all or the same sets of stimulus elements controlled in their environment. Increments of gain in stimulus adjustment in the child are matched in increments of stimulus exposure.

To reiterate, *none* of these characteristics which are so readily apparent and easily remembered when looking at a modified classroom *is an educational idea*. The totalities of modified features are only sets of conditions within which program ideas can be implemented for children who have basic auditory and/or visual perceptual pathology, and who need an environment adjusted to manageable form because of their inability to deal with it in conventional form. It should not be expected that any magic ensues simply from carpentry or interior design. An educational program must also exist.

In retrospect, it seems probable that a few teachers left the university with a memorized list of artifacts and forms without incorporating the rationale or the basic psychological issues relevant to the behavior of brain-injured children. A larger percentage of the administrators probably left the seminar with such a list rather than with an attitude or point of view.

Here it is very important to observe that in retrospect the teachers verbalized, almost without exception, the need for strong local support of their programs. The administrator who typically provides much of this support is the school principal. To commend teacher performance with a "pat on the back" may at times be needed. More often than not, however, it may be more detrimental than helpful if there is no reasonable basis for it.

Those teachers who are able to teach brain-injured children require relevant support. Intelligent dialogue about their program is basic to survival. "You're doing a fine job," as the format of support for a teacher who has some identified consultation needs, can be very threatening and can actually reinforce denial and distortion in the teacher. She may, in this instance, have the additional responsibility of making the program appear sound—whether it is or not. The demand on the teacher is great enough when she can accept her own needs and seek appropriate assistance; it is compounded when inappropriate "support" encourages her to deny or cover up deficiencies.

Part of this issue is involved in the administrator's feelings and expectations. If his expectations do not go beyond a quiet class-room where ripples are minimized, his responses and selection of support strategies will reflect this. If his orientation is to the forms and artifacts of the program, his responses will reflect this and his expectations of the program will most probably be entirely un-realistic. If his authority needs and his needs to appear technically competent and self-sufficient are related, he may tend to give easy unrealistic answers and pin responsibility for the answer on the teacher if it doesn't work because of faulty implementation. He may, on the other hand, fear exposure of incompetence, and reject the program and the teacher.

What the teacher needs is not an answer man but a comrade in the struggle for answers. She knows, or should know, that easy answers are not forthcoming. She needs help in identifying the is-sues and then, if indicated, assistance in obtaining the most appro-priate consultation. The issue may be technical or personal. It may only be the need for additional materials and supplies. This latter kind of support is extremely important but, unfortunately, to deliver every available device and piece of material to the door of the classroom is not sufficient support. Here the orientation to the forms and artifacts of the model will tend to reinforce this kind of support strategy. The "What can I buy for you?" in offering support to these teachers can be very important or terribly irrelevant.

WHEN THE CHIPS ARE DOWN

With the demands made on the teacher inside the classroom by the children, there is little energy to spare. Reserve energy or not, additional responsibilities exist. She must participate with other professionals in the assessment and placement of children. She must relate to parents—the nature of this relationship depending on the way the program is defined and the supporting personnel available. She must carry on dialogue with clinical staff as to the progress of the children, seeking their counsel. Because the program is usually new, she must continually describe and interpret. She must be particularly skilled and tactful in relating to other teachers in the same building. The extent and nature of these demands on her energy reserve, however, are in large measure determined by the buffering services provided by the administration. These services should control such factors as classroom open-door policies where visitors can come and go as they please; exploiting the teacher's special skills by expecting her to speak at every PTA, civic or professional meeting that has interest in special children; or automatically assigning her to membership on a myriad of committees just because they have some relationship to exceptional children. Her skills should be appropriately used in the system, but a protective attitude toward the teacher, where her commitments are determined by logical priorities (and her honest consent) rather than by assignment, is advisable.

The teacher's role in the school has been mentioned but needs some elaboration. Her relationship to other teachers in the building is important to her (and, whether they know it or not, to the regular class teachers as well). The kinds of issues that sometimes subvert positive interactions are often subtle and usually delicate.

The children in these classes are the ones who have not been able to function in regular classes. There are good reasons for this. Many of the children could not have functioned in any teacher's class of thirty or thirty-five with a regular curriculum. They require a special program or they would not be in the class, assuming they have been appropriately placed. This reality is not always appreciated. Regular class teachers, because they are human too, and like to see all children in their class succeed, are sometimes ambivalent and occasionally hostile toward a special teacher. The special teacher's job is to succeed with the children they could not help. The regular teachers sometimes feel threatened by the unwarranted inference that they have been inadequate to the task. Teachers such as these have some difficulty with the special teachers' comments, passing in the hall or in the teachers' lounge, which relate to the children's progress. (The special teacher may even be excited over some behavior elicited from a child during the morning. To whom does she then relate her sense of rare joy?) These same regular teachers may even experience anxiety reduction in instances where the children from their rooms are apparently not making progress in the special program.

We must hasten to add that this is not always the case, and probably not even the more typical case. This type of dynamic, however, may explain much of another type of case; the one which is most often stated as the source of negative interactions. The more typically described case goes something like this: "She has only eight children in her class. I have thirty-two. She makes as much money as I do. I have children in my class just like hers. I'm sure I could teach any children if I had only eight. Why does she need an aide with that little group?" And so goes the evaluation of the class and the teacher.

It is obvious that a job of explaining and interpreting has to be done. What may not be so obvious is the complexity of that job. There are usually strong feelings attached to these statements. When the chips are down, the burden of "proof" is on the special teacher. The justification of what superficially appear to be special benefits is laid on the special teacher. The magical expectations of some other teachers and some school officials (based on misunderstanding of the nature of the program or the children in it) serve to raise the special teacher's normal anxiety. She is outnumbered and surrounded. The realities of her professional environment cannot be ignored.

The authors observed in most cases that after the regular teachers became familiar with the problems of these children and the type of program the special teacher was operating, not one would have changed places with her. She then commanded respect and could actually be of some help to the other teachers.

The major payoff for the special teacher in this positive relationship with the faculty is a mutual feeling of membership on the faculty. To be accepted as a part of the faculty rather than an added feature is very important to the teacher. Psychological benefits accrue which help to combat the day-to-day tension, fatigue, and isolation, and pragmatic benefits accrue which pave the way for reintegration of pupils into regular classes.

More sophisticated regular teachers and sensitive principals are extremely helpful to the special teacher. They share in her joy, empathize with her disappointments, and support her when she is discouraged. That they are there and that they seem to care is often as important as their technical understanding.

MYSTIQUE, FUTILITY, AND ALIENATION

Some special teachers, unfortunately, never experience the fulfillment of working in a positive situation because the hurdles are insurmountable in attaining the type of camaraderie that has been described. Reasons for not combating mythology or sharing the nature of the program may be due to teacher immaturity. Professional peermanship is a condition that not all teachers achieve. Some may be particularly good with children but ineffective in working with adults.

Another reason may be that the demands in the special class are so great that the teacher does not have energy left over for this additional investment. Hence, a defensive, "I don't really care, just so I can do my job." The energy drain beyond energy resources may be due to several things: the teacher's own personal problems are absorbing her strength, the children in the class were unwisely placed or grouped, adequate administrative support is lacking, or any one of several other conditions may obtain. The fact is that the special teacher sometimes either refuses to try or blunders in her efforts to secure comfortable intraschool relationships.

All kinds of defensive strategies on the part of the special teacher may be observed in these circumstances. One is the use of the negative responses of the other teachers. Having said she doesn't care (although she almost always does), and dismissing her responsibility on the basis of "their ignorance," she proceeds to exploit the mystique set which often exists, especially in the beginning. She allows others to see her as practicing a high form of witchcraft. She does not interact with the other teachers, never frequents the teachers' lounge, faculty meetings (or if she is required to do so she keeps silent), or local professional meetings. When approached by a faculty member who inquires as to "how things are going" she may respond, "Oh, just fine;" or, an admiring "How do you do it?" may elicit: "It's all in a day's work."

The point to be made here is that effective program development may be substantially sabotaged by this kind of situation. Most often this teacher is alone, and more often than not in stress. To remain unapproachable and use herself in what she knows is an unrealistic way is self-defeating. The demands on the positive use of self are enormous. The negative use of self, even if in defense, is futile. The futility of this game and the inability to deliver the results demanded by the mystique usually limits her stay in that program. At most, she is usually there for one year.

With reaction formations of denial, displacement, projection, or whatever the character of the response, these teachers cannot continue to cope with what they perceive to be a hostile world and work effectively with brain-injured children at the same time.

MASOCHISTS OR MASTERS

It may be observed, and not entirely inappropriately, that the demands made on these teachers by the children are unrealistic. Why would they choose such work when they could make as much money (sometimes more) doing any number of other important jobs in education? Such a person must be asking for punishment. Maybe so. Certainly a myriad of motivations attract teachers to this field. The authors would not, however, accept the point of view that suggests these motivations must be poor or in any sense pathologic. Hopefully, a teacher carrying an excess freight of guilt causing her to solicit punishment will probably not find herself in the field very long. The healthiest of people are needed to teach these children. The weaknesses of the strongest will eventually come to the fore—if not visible to others, to the teachers themselves.

STRANGERS IN THE RIGHT

There has been much discussion of the problems of labeling and defining the children we are calling brain-injured. That multiple labels are used and vary according to the geographic location and professional orientation of the person using the label has been made clear. This issue continues to be confusing and perplexing and is yet to be brought under professional standards.

In following up the teachers and the programs that developed, the authors were impressed more and more with the importance and impact of the labeling jungle. In some systems, primarily because of historical reasons, the more clearly medically derived labels such as "brain damage," "brain injury," or "central nervous system disorder" were used, and the definition was largely agreed upon by those responsible for the program. In other systems the more descriptive, as opposed to explanatory, labels were used, such as "learning disability," "perceptually disturbed," or "hyperactive."

While no educational problems are solved simply by the use of one term or another, certain problems do arise with the use of certain labels. The use of the more medically derived ones can be problematic in educational settings, based on our observations, unless descriptive behavioral definitions are applied and accepted. Where the more descriptive, behaviorally oriented labels were used, a sense of closure existed because of the definitions implied. In either event, however, lack of clarity or definition existed in many instances. Much of this seemed to relate to territorial interests of different professional groups. It may not be an overstatement to suggest that the labeling issue is a smoke screen used to cloud other more basic issues. No matter what a child is called, open professional discussion of his needs can lead to effective programming. No child need be a stranger to any professional who works with children just because the label pinned to the coattail of his problems is new or different. He has a right to appropriate service that goes beyond the surface implications of that label.

PROFESSIONAL DISSOCIATION

The pathology observed in some children who see pieces and parts and cannot incorporate the whole seems analogous to what we observe in professional interactions. The we-they, mine-yours focus, if pushed too far, can force us into maintaining tunnel vision and never to incorporate significant larger issues.

The imperative that educators join forces with other professionals in understanding and serving children who have exceptional needs is not an academic issue. The logic of such an approach is as definitive as the erasure of mind-body, intellect-affect, cause-effect, symptom-cause, nature-nurture, and other dichotomies. It is as urgent as the manpower deficit. Its need is indicated by the state of our knowledge. Such an approach, however, must take seriously several realities. Service has been segmented. Professional groups have owned domains or territories of concern by virtue of their historical responsibility for dealing with them. Language systems have emerged within these ranks which deter communication and cloud areas of common concern.

It was the authors' observation that these problems were not automatically solved even in situations where, in good faith, there was expressed agreement that such an approach was indicated. Certainly in those situations where there was an intellectual meeting of the minds and some commitment to the idea of cooperative effort and shared responsibility, the process of effective interdisciplinary activity was soundly launched. In every case someone had to take active leadership. It does not seem reasonable to wait until all parts are completely ready before beginning work on developing the whole; in this case, collaborative effort.

Effective interdisciplinary action is often sabotaged by personal feelings of threat or pride. "What does he know about education, he has never taught a day in his life," or "Well, how should he know; he only sees the child an hour at a time," or "What good does it do to write up a report on this child for the school? It won't be used and if it is they won't know what to do with it," or "How do they expect to help those children? No one is doing anything to help with the home situation." These and other similar statements are familiar to all of us and are so much a part of our everyday work that we do not think twice about their meaning.

The fact is that each statement may be true. There are two assumptions, however, that can typically be tied to each statement, both of which are probably false. One is that the other person is either naive or stupid. The other is that the person making the statement shares no responsibility for remedying the situation.

In the first case the other person may simply be uninformed. A job of education is obviously required in this instance. To take some responsibility for this job is, of course, to negate the second assumption, in which case, the statement probably would not have been made.

This, too, is oversimplified and can even be dangerous. To assume responsibility for informing or "educating" the other in the sense of indoctrinating him to our point of view is an affront to the other's intelligence and integrity. Constructive mutual education is stymied until we are able to take the initiative in offering to help and at the same time solicit help, to start with the attitude of a learner as well as a teacher, to be as open to change in one's own self and belief system or point of view as one demands in the other. We should not be deluded, however, that aggression is always the better part of valor when the sound development of trust and professional maturity are left aside.

Conclusions

Because of the singularity of theoretical orientation and the deliberate effort to sensitize teachers to a particular body of literature and method, it continued to seem reasonable to assume that the teachers left the teaching program with at least that much in common. The teachers did have familiarity with similar concepts, access to and knowledge of certain materials, and awareness of the kinds of questions that could be raised about the behavior of brain-injured and hyperactive children in order to establish an educational program. Beyond this technical base of commonality, however, major differences became apparent. The acquisition of technical competence did not necessarily insure use of the point of view upon which such skills were based. A few teachers, because of previous training and experience, because of reasonable disagreement, because of personality, because of in-training experiences which served as negative reinforcers, or for any number of other factors, did not implement the kind of educational program to which they were exposed in training. For the teachers as a group, when they returned to their systems with intentions of implementing an educational program they did not enter vacuums. Each teacher returned to an established school system. Each system had its own philosophy of education, its own attitude toward exceptional children, its own history in providing special services, its own administrative organization. Some had more money than others. Some had one or more aggressive leaders in special education who could provide guidance at a system level. Some had sophisticated pupil personnel services. At the local school level, some of the principals of schools in which classes were housed were more informed and more actively supportive of the teacher and the program than others.

Although each school system had a representative attend the administrators' seminar in an effort to supply the authority and decision-making channels with adequate information to support the program, the individuality of system resources, organization and momentum was maintained. Also, the administrators who attended the seminars had varying degrees of ability and interest which affected the extent to which they could use the seminar experience.

In summary, while the teachers who went through the training program emerged with some common information and skills, their differences in implementation potential probably were greater than their similarities. Most certainly the school systems to which they returned were decidedly different, each with its own challenges, problems, and potential for support.

This situation obviously makes generalization difficult. It also serves to document the observation made earlier that the training program could not be viewed as a treatment and evaluated from that point of view without major qualification. Case study information presented in the evaluation is probably the more useful and valid.

The authors quickly came to the same conclusion as Gallagher [3], who raised serious questions about the pre-test—treatment—post-test design in teacher training. As has been pointed out, while the program was designed to train teachers in one approach to the education of brain-injured children, it could not be viewed as a treatment entity with consistent and carefully defined parameters. The train-observe design, while limited in the production of "hard data" which all feel more comfortable in sharing, is one strategy for inquiry. It accepts the reality, which in fact existed, that the programs established in local school systems were not singular in identity but rather Xeon-Utah-Syracuse, Yules-Florida-Syracuse, Zorba-Texas-Syracuse, that is, only in part resembling the model to which the teachers were exposed.

The implications of this observation are far-reaching. First, any assumption of one-to-one relationship between university training and programs established in local school systems was not borne out in the authors' experience. Even though calculated efforts (already described) were made to ensure as much continuity as possible, these existed only to a very limited degree.

Whether the program model is feasible or not, it is one proposal for an educational strategy, with some support of evidence, for working with one clinically defined group of exceptional children. It requires the acceptance of the reality that such children exist and need service. It further proposes a program or content for that service. In one sense the market demand-supply model is relevant. The existence and need of these children has been coming into focus since the late forties. By no means can it be said, however, that school administrators fully accept this and rank the needs of these children as a top priority item in their over-all programs. The demand of an identified market is not yet completely formulated. In actual fact, the supply of trained teachers was not incorporated with equal absorption into the market that does exist. Some systems were ready to establish programs on the day the teacher completed her training. Others were slow in establishing programs for various reasons. Some of the systems utilized the teachers in non-teaching situations such as supervisory and administrative positions. Some were used in relation to other exceptionalities because of the level of program differentiation existing in the system.

One way of viewing this situation is from the point of view of change. That is, how can innovation be introduced most effectively? That trained teachers were not readily and appropriately absorbed in all instances would suggest that the clarity with which the need has been articulated is variable, as would be expected.

A more important observation, however, is that teacher training programs must examine their strategies in terms of logistical assumption. The Syracuse program paid attention to content issues by orienting a program convergently based on the assumption that if teachers had a clear, in-depth exposure to one approach, they could with some ease implement a program utilizing this frame of reference. The realities of local school system administration were only partially acknowledged by conducting the administrators' seminars, and the dimensions of this reality were not entirely appreciated and accounted for in the training strategy.

Teacher training at the university level, whether of teachers of brain-injured children or of children with some other exceptionality, should, in the authors' opinions, involve the local school systems more basically in the training process. The logistics of local school system involvement must be worked out with invention and in- genuity. The problem of bridging the gap between the hallowed halls of ivy, where ideas and innovations are frequently articulated in theoretical form, and the classroom, where the job of education is in process, is basic (obviously ideas and action both happen at both places but the picture is overdrawn here to make an important point). Keeping research and training functions in the exclusive domain of universities, while placing the task of educating children in the exclusive domain of teachers, supervisors and administrators, is a functional distinction that is making less and less sense. If the challenge now facing all special educators is to be met squarely, the innovators, the teachers, the researchers, the administrators and supervisors must find ways of sharing responsibilities for train- ing and education. Breakdowns in feedback relating to ideas for education and the realities of classroom and system problems is a luxury indulged in only at the expense of developing quality pro- grams. The university professor should be concerned with the communication complex in the local school, with the fiscal realities of the system, and with the philosophical points of view of the administrators. The principals, supervisors, directors, assistant superintendents, and superintendents must be no less concerned with the problems of training teachers, the issues in educational research and the problems of innovation. The consultation model for bridging informational, service, and manpower gaps needs to be developed more extensively than it has been in the past. In this particular instance the suggestion is that consultation should go in both directions.

Based on observations of many systems, the authors would sug- gest that the process of developing a shared responsibility and mutuality of effort must proceed in terms of developing basic rela- tionships, and this, when one calls a spade a spade, essentially is based on developing trust. It is not enough that a professor get into a school classroom; he must be trusted there. It is not sufficient to have school officials on committees advisory to training programs, and teaching some courses; their opinions should be actively sought and differences of opinion resolved through candid dialogue based on mutual respect.

The idealism in this point of view is obvious. The essentiality of this type of effort is, to the authors, imperative.

The large university training and research center still has a major role to play. The role of more localized and regional training efforts, however, needs to be explored in depth. Only in this sense can training and evaluation begin to take the form of two operations belonging to the same process.

REFERENCES

1. R. J. Schaefer, *The School as a Center of Inquiry* (New York: Harper & Row, 1967), 33–34.

2. F. Redl, *When We Deal With Children* (New York: The Free Press, 1966), 15.

3. James J. Gallagher, "New Directions in Special Education," *Exceptional Children* (March, 1967), 441–47.

SELECTED BIBLIOGRAPHY

GENERAL EDUCATION

The American Association of Colleges for Teacher Education. *Strength Through Reappraisal,* Sixteenth Yearbook, The American Association of Colleges for Teacher Education, Proceedings of the 1963 Annual Meeting. Washington: The Association, 1963.

Barr, A. S. and Singer, A., Jr. "Evaluative Studies of Teacher Education," *Journal of Teacher Education,* IV (1953), 65–72.

Benson, A. L. "The Role of Examinations in the Preparation of Teachers," *Journal of Teacher Education,* X (December, 1959), 491–96.

Bestor, A. E. "On the Education and Certification of Teachers," *School and Society,* LXXVIII (September 19, 1953), 81–86.

Broudy, H. S. "Can We Save Teacher Education From Its Enemies and Friends?" *Strength Through Reappraisal,* Sixteenth Yearbook, The American Association of Colleges for Teacher Education, Proceedings of the 1963 Annual Meeting. Washington: The Association, 1963.

Broudy, H. S. "Criteria for the Professional Preparation of Teachers, in Symposium on the Education of Teachers in America," *Journal of Teacher Education,* XVI (December, 1965), 408–15.

Brubacher, J. S. "Teacher Education: Development," *Encyclopedia of Educational Research,* Edited by C. W. Harris. 3d ed. New York: The Macmillan Co., 1960.

Cushman, M. L. "Organization and Administration of Teacher Education," *The Education of Teachers: New Perspectives.* National Commission on Teacher Education and Professional Standards. Washington: National Education Association, 1958.

Drake, W. E. "Introduction, in Symposium on the Education of Teachers in America," *Journal of Teacher Education,* XVI (December, 1965).

Ebel, R. L. "Measurement Applications in Teacher Education: A Review of Relevant Research," *Journal of Teacher Education,* XVII (Spring, 1966), 15–25.

Eibling, H. H. "Education for a New Century," *Education,* LXXXVI (January, 1966), 259–62.

Evendon, E. S. "Twenty-five Years of Teacher Education," *Educational Record,* XXIII (October, 1943), 334–44.

Fischer, J. H. "The Prospect in Teacher Education, in Symposium on the Education of Teachers in America," *Journal of Teacher Education,* XVI (December, 1965).

198

Glennon, V. J. *The Road Ahead in Teacher Education.* The 1957 J. Richard Street Lecture, Syracuse University School of Education. Syracuse: Syracuse University Press, 1957.

"Improvement of Teacher Education; Research at University of Texas and Stanford University," *School and Society,* XCIII (November 27, 1965), 442–43.

Johnson, W. H. "Preparing to Teach; Past Practices, Current Trends in Ohio," *The Clearing House,* XL (December, 1965), 206–209.

Koerner, J. D. "Theory and Experiment in the Education of Teachers," *Strength Through Reappraisal,* Sixteenth Yearbook, The American Association of Colleges for Teacher Education, Proceedings of the 1963 Annual Meeting. Washington: The Association, 1963.

Krathwohl, D. R. "Study of the Arkansas Experiment in Teacher Education," *The Future Challenges Teacher Education,* Eleventh Yearbook, The American Association of Colleges for Teacher Education, Proceedings of the 1958 Annual Meeting. Chicago: The Association, 1958.

Krathwohl, D. and Spalding, W. B. "Evaluation of the Arkansas Experiment in Teacher Education," *Journal of Teacher Education,* VII (September, 1956), 233–35.

Masoner, P. H. *A Design for Teacher Education.* Horace Mann Lecture, 1963. Pittsburgh: University of Pittsburgh Press, 1963.

McAulay, J. D. "The Preparation of Elementary Teachers in the Social Studies," *Journal of Teacher Education,* XVII (Spring, 1966), 89–92.

National Commission on Teacher Education and Professional Standards. *The Education of Teachers: New Perspectives.* Washington: National Education Association, 1958.

The National Society of College Teachers of Education. *The Education of Teachers,* Twenty-third Yearbook, The National Society of College Teachers of Education. Chicago: The University of Chicago Press, 1935.

Pomeroy, E. C. "The Continuing Quest," *Foundations for Excellence.* Fifteenth Yearbook, The American Association of Colleges for Teacher Education, Proceedings of the 1962 Annual Meeting. Chicago: The Association, 1962.

Prall, C. E. *State Programs for the Improvement of Teacher Education.* Washington: American Council on Education, 1946.

Snider, G. R. and Long, D. "Are Teacher Education Programs Attracting Academically Able Students?" *Journal of Teacher Education,* XII (December, 1961), 407–11.

Stiles, L. J. "The All-Institution Approach to Teacher Education," *The Education of Teachers: New Perspectives,* National Commission on Teacher Education and Professional Standards. Washington: National Education Association, 1958.

Stiles, L. J., Barr, A. S., Douglass, H. R., and Mills, H. H. *Teacher Education in the United States.* New York: The Ronald Press Co., 1960.

Stinnett, T. M. and Clarke, C. M. "Teacher Education: Programs," *Encyclopedia of Educational Research*. Edited by C. W. Harris. 3d ed. New York: The Macmillan Co., 1960.

Trout, D. M. *The Education of Teachers*. Lansing, Mich.: The Michigan Cooperative Teacher Education Study, 1943.

U.S. Office of Education. *Education in the U.S.A.* U.S. Department of Health, Education, and Welfare, Office of Education. Washington: U.S. Government Printing Office, 1960.

U.S. Office of Education. *The National Survey of the Education of Teachers*. Vols. V, VI. U.S. Office of Education Bulletin No. 10, 1933. Washington: U.S. Government Printing Office, 1933.

Woodring, P. *New Directions in Teacher Education*. New York: Fund for the Advancement of Education, 1957.

Woodring, P. "The New Look in Teacher Education, *The Future Challenges Teacher Education*, The American Association of Colleges for Teacher Education, Eleventh Yearbook, Proceedings of the 1958 Annual Meeting. Chicago: The Association, 1958.

SPECIAL EDUCATION

Balow, B. "The Emotionally and Socially Handicapped," *Review of Educational Research*, XXXVI (February, 1966), 120–33.

Cain, L. "Special Education," *Encyclopedia of Educational Research*, Edited by C. W. Harris. 3d ed. New York: The Macmillan Co., 1930.

Claytor, Mae P. "State Certification Requirements for Teachers of Atypical Children," *Journal of Genetic Psychology*, LXXX (1952), 211–20.

Cruickshank, W. M. "New Horizons in Teacher Preparation: The President's Message," *Exceptional Children*, XIX (1952), 89–91.

Cruickshank, W. M. "Teacher Education and Exceptional Children," *Exceptional Children*, XIX (1952), 1–2.

DeRidder, L. M. "Education for Teachers of Handicapped Children," *Elementary School Journal*, L (1950), 521–29.

Dockrell, W. B. "Preparing Teachers of Handicapped Children in Canada," *Journal of Teacher Education*, XIII (1962), 110–11.

Elledge, Lela M. "Present Requirements for Teachers of Sub-Normal and Superior Children," *Elementary School Journal*, XXIX (December, 1928), 303–306.

Featherstone, W. B. "Preparation of Special Education Teachers: Administrative Problems," *Education*, LXX (1950), 460–65.

Hill, A. C. "Preparing Teachers for Exceptional Children," *Crippled Child*, XXVII (1949), 16–17, 30.

Miller, C. A. A. J. "What Kind of Qualifications and Training Should the Teacher of the Special Class Have?" *Journal of Addresses and Proceedings of the N.E.A. of the U.S.*, XLVIII (1910) (Boston, Mass.), 1061–65.

Murphy, F. W. "Preparation of Special Education Teachers: Basic Concepts and Principles," *Education*, LXX (March, 1950), 455–59

Parker, Rose E. "Undergraduate Preparation for Teachers of Exceptional Children," *Sight-saving Review*, XVIII (1948), 63–69.

Rabinow, B. "A Training Program for Teachers of the Emotionally Disturbed and the Socially Maladjusted," *Exceptional Children*, XXVI (February, 1960), 287–93.

Taylor, W. W. and Taylor, Isabelle W. "The Education of Special Teachers in Western Europe," *Journal of Teacher Education*, XII (1961), 192–200.

U.S. Department of Health, Education, and Welfare. *College and University Programs for the Preparation of Teachers of Exceptional Children.* Washington, 1954. U.S. Office of Education Bulletin No. 13, 1954.

U.S. Department of Health, Education, and Welfare. *State Certification Requirements for Teachers of Exceptional Children.* Washington, 1954. U.S. Office of Education Bulletin No. 1, 1954.

U.S. Department of Health, Education, and Welfare. *Teachers of Children Who are Socially and Emotionally Maladjusted.* Washington, 1957. U.S. Office of Education Bulletin No. 11, 1957.

Wallin, J. E. W. "The Baltimore Plan of Training Special Class Teachers and Other Workers in the Field of Special Education," *Elementary School Journal*, XXXI (April, 1931), 607–18.

Wallin, J. E. W. "Trends and Needs in the Training of Teachers for Special Classes for Handicapped Children," *Journal of Educational Research*, XXXI (March, 1938), 506–26.

Wilson, C. C. "Preparation of Teachers for the Education of the Exceptional," *Journal of Exceptional Children*, XIII (October, 1946), 17–18, 30.

Wozniak, J. M. "Teacher Training for Special Education," *National Catholic Educational Association Bulletin*, LVII (1960), 425–28.

OTHER RELATED REFERENCES

Allen, E. A. "Professional Training of Teachers: A Review of Research," *Educational Research*, V (June, 1963), 200–15.

American Association of Colleges for Teacher Education. *The Future Challenges to Teacher Education.* Oneonta: The Association, 1958.

Blackman, L. S. "A Study of Survey Courses on the Exceptional Child," *Exceptional Children*, XXIV (1958), 194–97.

Blackmore, Dorothy S. "Preparing Teachers for the Educationally Handicapped," *Academic Therapy Quarterly*, I (1965), 28–30.

Doll, E. A. "The Next Ten Years in Special Education," *Training School Bulletin*, XXIV (February, 1928), 145–53.

"Education of Teachers in America: Symposium," *Journal of Teacher Education*, XVI (December, 1965), 389–426.

French, J. L. "Trends in the Preparation of Teachers of the Gifted," *Exceptional Children*, XXXII (December, 1965), 255–56.

Haskew, L. D. "The Real Story in Teacher Education," *Journal of Teacher Education*, IX (June, 1958), 124–26.

Higgins, L. C. "Teacher Training," *Austin Child Limited*, II (1964), 79–81.

Kelly, Elizabeth M. "The Teachers' College, Columbia, Pre-Service Program," *American Journal of Mental Deficiency*, LI (1947), 686–90.

Kelly, W. F. "Current Trends in Requirements for Teacher Certification: Dangers to the Colleges," *National Catholic Educational Association Bulletin*, LII (August, 1955), 219–22.

Keppel, F. "Contemporary Issues in the Education of Teachers," *Journal of Teacher Education*, III (December, 1952), 249–55.

Mayor, J. R. *et al.* "Implications for Teacher Education of Recent Research in Math Education," *Journal of Teacher Education*, XVI (December, 1965), 483–90.

National Commission on Teacher Education and Professional Standards. *The Education of Teachers: New Perspectives*. Washington: National Education Association, 1958.

National Commission on Teacher Education and Professional Standards. *Teacher Education: The Decade Ahead*. Washington: National Education Association, 1955.

Parker, Rose E. "Educating the Teacher of Exceptional Children," *Illinois Education*, XXXII (May, 1944), 267–68, 285–86.

Rowell, H. G. "The Opportunities Which the University Offers for the Training of Teachers of Handicapped Children," *Volta Review*, XXXI (October, 1929), 613–20.

Scholl, G. T. and Milazzo, T. C. "Federal Program in the Preparation of Professional Personnel in the Education of Handicapped Children and Youth," *Exceptional Children*, XXXII (November, 1965), 157–64.

Shaplin, J. T. "Harvard Internship Program for the Preparation of Elementary and Secondary School Teachers," *Educational Record*, XXXVII (March, 1957), 316–25.

Smith, J. G. "Training Teachers for Specialized Education," *Texas Outlook*, XXXII (1948), 18–19.

Steward, L. "A Study of Critical Training Requirements for Teaching Success," *Journal of Educational Research*, XLIX (May, 1956), 651–61.

Stiles, L. J. "Teacher Education: An All-University Function," *School and Society*, LXII (October 6, 1945), 220–22.

Stout, Ruth A. "Selective Admission and Retention Practices in Teacher Education," *Journal of Teacher Education*, VIII (September, 1957; December, 1965), 299–317, 423–32.

"Training of Teachers of Handicapped Children in New York State College for Teachers, Buffalo," *School and Society*, LXV (June 28, 1947), 472–73.

Tyach, D. "History of Education and the Preparation of Teachers: A Reappraisal," *Journal of Teacher Education,* XVI (December, 1965), 427–31.

U.S. Office of Education. *Opportunity for the Preparation of Teachers of Exceptional Children.* Chicago: National Society for Crippled Children and Adults, 1949.

White, Verna. "Selection of Prospective Teachers at Syracuse University," *Journal of Teacher Education,* I (March, 1950), 24–31.

Wiseman, S. and Start, K. B. "Follow-up of Teachers Five Years after Completing Their Training," *British Journal of Educational Psychology,* XXXV (November, 1965), 342–61.